AM

LES

THE OFFICIAL BOOK OF THE 2005 SIX NATIONS CHAMPIONS

BREATHING FIRE!

Living the Grand Slam dream with Wales' rugby heroes

In loving memory of Leanne Harry and Toby Lloyd Cockbain

TEAM
WALES

VSP

HUW EVANS
Picture Agency Cardiff

CONTENTS

Welcome to the official 2005 Six Nations book of Team Wales...

Wow! When our journey started back in the New Year, none of us could ever have expected or imagined anything like this. We started the season as one of the outsiders to win the RBS Six Nations Championship and we ended the campaign with five wins from as many games and a hat-trick of titles. So I hope this book gives an indication, both in words and pictures, of what the party endured and enjoyed over that amazing six week period.

You dream of a Triple Crown, Championship or Grand Slam and of course you hope and pray that after so many promising starts you can find a way of adding the end result. But at the beginning of this particular Six Nations Championship, most of us simply craved an end to the disappointing run that had brought us close but not close enough during last autumn's series of games.

Like any other Welshman or woman, you imagine what it would feel like to stand on the rostrum, holding aloft £60,000 worth of silver trophy. But the reality is that after so many years of relative failure, you find it hard to think any further than that next game. And that, in the end, was our strength. Although it remains as one of the sport's great cliches, during the 2005 Six Nations Championship we kept telling ourselves to concentrate on one game at a time and to avoid getting ahead of ourselves. Any other approach would have been tantamount to sporting suicide.

Personally, I was greatly honoured last year when Mike Ruddock gave me an opportunity to captain my country. Firstly, I felt quite humble for I never expected anything like this. I would go as far as saying that I was honoured and proud just to be part of the squad, but to be captain of such a young squad with such potential and desire made it even more special.

And as our glorious Six Nations campaign unfolded, the people who had spent so long chastising us and criticising our results began to change their tune and to see that potential. In the end, the Grand Slam proved those people wrong. It was our way of shoving it down the throats of our band of critics.

For me the championship went a little pear-shaped in France, but that apart it was as near perfect as anyone could ever have hoped for. Beating England was fantastic, gaining revenge in Rome for two years ago was satisfying, winning in Paris and Edinburgh was wonderful and then to finish up in Cardiff by beating the pre-competition favourites was simply beyond belief.

Last but not least, I'd like to use this fantastic book to give a message to the fans from me and all the boys. Thanks for your support, not only this season, but over the past few years when winning Grand Slams or Triple Crowns has proved to be nothing more than a pipe dream. This success was just reward for our efforts, and for the supporters who have followed us through thick and thin, in the hope one day that we would find ourselves sitting on top of the European pile, thanks - you're all part of this very special team.

Croeso i lyfr swyddogol tîm Cymru ar bencampwriaeth y chwe gwlad 2005...

Wow! Pan gychwynnodd ein taith ni nôl ar ddechrau'r flwyddyn newydd, allai'r un ohonon ni fyth fod wedi disgwyl na dychmygu y gallai unrhyw beth tebyg i hyn ddigwydd.

Doedd neb yn rhoi unrhyw obaith i ni ennill Pencampwriaeth R.B.S. y Chwe Gwlad, a nawr dyma ni wedi gorffen yr ymgyrch wedi ennill pob un o'n pum gêm, ac wedi cipio'r tlysau i gyd. Gobeithio y bydd y gyfrol hon, ar air ac mewn llun, yn rhoi rhyw gipolwg i bawb o'r hyn y bu'r garfan drwyddo yn y chwe wythnos rhyfeddol rheini; y dioddef, y dathlu, a'r mwynhad.

Wrth gwrs mae dyn bob amser yn breuddwydio am ennill Coron Driphlyg, Pencampwriaeth, neu hyd yn oed Gamp Lawn; ac yn gweddïo, ar ôl dechrau'n addawol mor aml, y gellid cael y canlyniad iawn hefyd o'r diwedd. Ond yr unig beth ym meddyliau'r chwaraewyr i gyd ar ddechrau'r Bencampwriaeth oedd gweld diwedd ar y rhediad siomedig oedd wedi dod â ni mor agos, ond nid yn ddigon agos, yng nghyfres gemau'r hydref. Rydw i, fel unrhyw Gymro neu Gymraes arall, wedi ceisio dyfalu droeon sut deimlad fyddai sefyll ar y llwyfan a dal yn uchel y tlws arian gwerth 60,000 o bunnoedd i bawb gael ei weld. Ond y realiti, ar ôl cymaint o dymhorau o fethiant cymharol, oedd ei chael hi'n anodd edrych ymhellach ymlaen na'r gêm nesaf. Ond hynny, yn y diwedd, oedd ein cryfder. Rwy'n gwybod ei bod hi'n hen ystrydeb, ond dyna beth roedden ni'n ei ddweud yn gyson wrth ein gilydd; canolbwyntio ar y gêm nesaf yn unig, a pheidio edrych ymhellach na hynny. Byddai unrhyw agwedd arall wedi bod yn llawer rhy beryglus.

Yn bersonol roeddwn i'n ei hystyried hi'n fraint enfawr y llynedd pan ofynnodd Mike Ruddock i fi fod yn gapten ar y tîm. Teimlwn yn wylaidd iawn, gan nad oeddwn wedi disgwyl dim byd o'r fath. Gallwn fynd mor bell â dweud fy mod i'n ei hystyried hi'n anrhydedd fawr dim ond i fod yn aelod o'r garfan. Ond roedd cael bod yn gapten ar garfan mor ifanc, ac oedd mor llawn awydd ac addewid, hyd yn oed yn bwysicach i fi. Ond wrth i'n tymor rhyfeddol ni yn y Chwe Gwlad ddatblygu, dechreuodd y rheini oedd wedi bod mor feirniadol o'n canlyniadau ni newid eu cân, a chydnabod y potensial. Yn y diwedd, fe brofodd y Gamp Lawn pa mor anghywir fu barn y beirniaid hynny. Dyna'n ffordd ni o wneud iddyn nhw fwyta'u geiriau, a chydnabod y cam.

O safbwynt personol, fe aeth pethau o chwith i fi ym Mharis, ond ar wahân i hynny, roedd mor berffaith ag y gallai neb obeithio amdano. Roedd curo Lloeger yn ffantastig; talu'r pwyth yn ôl yn Rhufain am yr hyn ddigwyddodd ddwy flynedd yn ôl yn rhoi boddhad mawr; ennill ym Mharis a Chaeredin yn wych; ac yna coroni'r cwbwl drwy guro'r Gwyddelod, ffefrynnau pawb am y Bencampwriaeth ymlaen llaw, y tu hwnt i'n breuddwydion penna ni. Bu'n dymor i'w drysori.

Ac un neges ola cyn cloi i'r cefnogwyr. Diolch o galon am eich cefnogaeth, nid yn unig y tymor hwn, ond dros y blynyddoedd diwetha hefyd pan nad oedd y Bencampwriaeth a'r Gamp Lawn yn ddim mwy na breuddwyd ffôl. Roedd y llwyddiant eleni yn wobr deilwng i ni fel carfan am ein holl ymdrechion caled, ac i'r cefnogwyr am barhau i fod mor deyrngar i ni hyd yn oed drwy'r dyddiau blin, yn y gobaith y bydden ni eto, ryw ddydd, yn cael ein coroni'n Bencampwyr Ewrop. Rydych chi i gyd yn rhan o dîm arbennig iawn.

wales v england

saturday, 5th february, 2005

The allotments next to Pontyclun Rugby Club provide the unlikely backdrop for preparations for the arrival of England

Alfie antics: the skipper relieves the mounting pressure

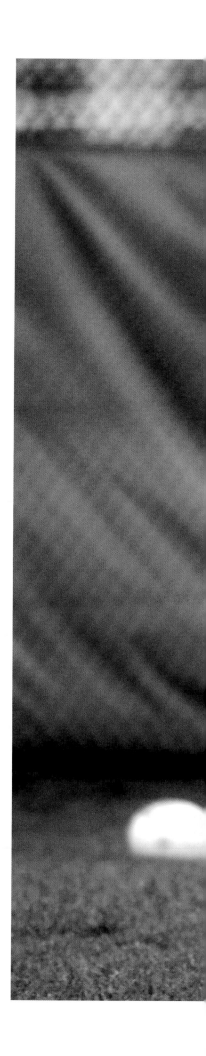

Ear we go: Brent Cockbain and Robin McBryde tape up for battle

"We're still looking for some of them!" Kit man John Rowlands helps Ceri Sweeney with kicking practice

A 74,000 strong choir gets ready to give England a noisy welcome

On the verge of history: Olympian Dame Tanni Grey-Thompson joins the boys for the national anthem

wales v england

Having punched the air with delight after realising my boyhood dream of scoring against England, I turned around to hear Alfie screaming, "There's nothing to be scared of, we can beat them." And it was from that moment that I honestly felt he was right.

It was an unbelievable feeling, almost crazy. As everyone knows in Wales, there is intense rivalry between the two nations - there always has been, especially on the rugby field. As a kid growing up with your mates in the valleys, you fantasise about scoring against England. I remember playing in the street, I used to score the winning try every day. Little did I know that one day I'd do it for real.

An hour later the final whistle went and the stadium was going wild and so were we. It was a truly amazing feeling, although at that stage we didn't know what lay ahead. I personally didn't believe it could get any better than that. There I was having beaten England for the first time and having scored a try, yet six weeks later that victory would pale into insignificance.

To be honest, such was the elation that the victory itself didn't sink in straight after the game, not for a few days in fact. When it did, however, I had to pinch myself. I couldn't believe that I had contributed to the victory - me Shane Williams from the Amman Valley, who so many people had written off for one reason or another.

Gavin Henson is so laid back I think he's going to topple over, but his contribution on the field against England was immense. The kick aside, his tackle on Matthew Tait was a significant point in the game. All week we had been reading the English journalists talking about this great player from Newcastle and how he was going to be unleashed on the Welsh. Well, he wasn't that effective on his back, and when Gavin dumped him there for the first time I think we all grew in confidence. It certainly struck a blow for the Welsh.

After that the self belief grew and grew, and when Gav popped it over with a few minutes remaining there was no way we were going to lose. It was our day. My first win against England, never to be forgotten.

SHANE WILLIAMS

Gareth Cooper (*left*) gets the backs moving and Michael Owen makes the hard yards

It seems like an eternity since I was dressed up in my old Wales jersey watching a Wales v England game in front of the television, nursing a bag of crisps and a can of coke back home in Tumble. If I was lucky, my father would swap the front room of our house for an afternoon in front of the big screen down at the local rugby club. Now that was a real treat - a day out with the boys!

I was no different to any other young lad growing up. I loved my country and loved to watch them play. However, when it came to the annual game against England it was extra special. It was a red letter day on the calendar, a day when we would hopefully put one over on the old enemy.

Personally, nothing much has changed now. I still wear the shirt and I still look forward with a certain relish to playing against them, it's just that now I find myself on the other side of the television screen.

Because of my passionate Welsh upbringing and my passion for everything Welsh, this season's game against England should have been like any other. In a way it was, but not in the way that most of our supporters felt. For them it was about beating England and enjoying the weekend. For us as players it was about bringing to an end a dreadful run of 'nearly but not quite' results against the best teams in the world. We can hide as much as we like behind a brave face and a few words of consolation for our performances in those big games in the autumn, but deep down losing by a point or a score hurt, it really hurt. To get so close and to lose out is almost as bad as suffering a significant loss.

So it wasn't so much about beating England, it was more about just winning - the opposition on this occasion was irrelevant. Well, at least that's what we told ourselves in the build up to the game.

The feeling in the dressing room before the England match was, therefore, rather tense. I remember looking around the room and thinking that there were not too many cool heads about.

Then, as we stood there singing the national anthem, wondering whether this would be the day, you could feel the tension rising. A lot of things had been said in the build up to the game about Wales going in as favourites and how England would struggle this season because of a glut of injuries and so many retirements after their World Cup triumph. We read and digested all the comments and, to be honest, spat them out. It didn't matter what anyone thought, it didn't matter who were the favourites, it was about us on the day - about taking that extra step to ensure victory.

We held each other pretty tight that February evening, then, as the crowd celebrated the anthem with us, and I knew from previous experience that as the band struck up, some of the guys were going to really struggle with their emotions. On this occasion some of those guys were probably too tight to sing, but it felt as emotional as ever. The support was magnificent and we were raring to get at them.

The rest, as they say, is history, and thankfully we finally conquered that most difficult of hurdles. All the years of waiting, years of hope, and hours, days and months of desperate hard work had brought its reward. To be truthful the performance itself, in our eyes, could have been better, but at the time that was insignificant.

To their credit, England took it well and we were able to sit back, albeit momentarily, to enjoy what had been a wonderful afternoon for us all. I spoke to a few of the England lads after the game and they didn't have a lot to say, just a few words about their impending coach journey back home.

For us, there were one or two drinks and a chance to reflect on the result. However, by the time it rolled on towards midnight I think most of us were tucked up in bed and looking ahead at Italy.

The roller-coaster was under way and we were strapping ourselves in for one hell of a ride.

DWAYNE PEEL

Dafydd Jones takes an unconventional route to
deal with Danny Grewcock before Alfie joins in

Eyes down: Martyn Williams surveys the England pack

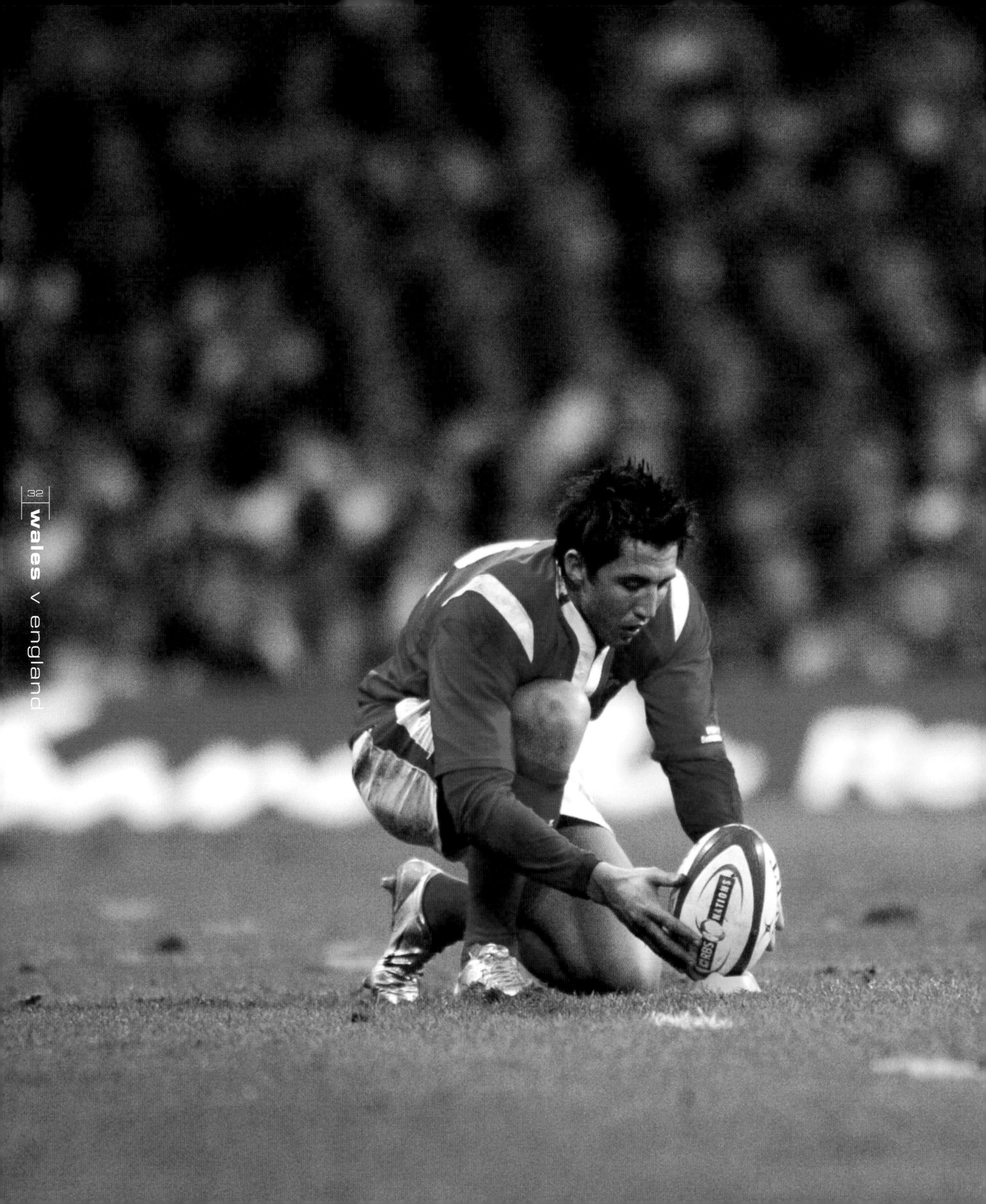
NATIONS

First of all let's set the record straight here. When we got the penalty I didn't pinch the ball off Stephen Jones or tell Alfie that I wanted a go. Mike had decided long before this campaign had started that I would be taking the long kicks, so I was more or less told that I was taking the kick.

And to be honest I was more than happy about that. I knew I could kick it. The only question was whether or not we should go for the corner, but Alfie just threw me the ball and said, "Go on Gav, have a go."

So I made sure that I teed it up properly, took one last look at the posts and told myself not to kick it too hard. As soon as I had made contact, I turned away. I always knew it would reach, it was just a case of getting the direction. Thankfully within the first few yards I realised it was spot on course.

From that moment on the spotlight fell on me and it wasn't really fair because it was a team effort. That kick was just one part of that game.

GAVIN HENSON

Four steps to heaven: Gavin kicks the winner against England

I can't remember which came first - was it the letter from the WRU telling me I was in the squad for the England game or the phone message from our team manager Alan Phillips saying 'well done'?

Anyway, it doesn't matter because from the moment I found out I had my head in the clouds. I kept asking myself 'is it a dream?' John Yapp, the ex-carpenter from Llantwit Major is going to be on the bench at least for the England game. I still pinch myself, just in case I am still sleeping and dreaming it all up.

I was tired of hearing the boys at Cardiff saying that playing for Wales was like a dream coming true. They all say it. You know the kind of thing.

"When I was growing up, all I wanted to do was play for Wales."

Well, guess what I said to the first press man I spoke to after getting the nod?

"When I was growing up, the only thing I wanted to do was play for Wales."

He looked at me a bit gone out, as if to say, 'well, I knew you were going to say that'. But to be honest, I couldn't think of anything else.

From the moment I read it on the letter and heard Alan's message, it felt so good. Obviously there was plenty of hard work to do once I teamed up with the boys, but just to be around them and working towards the same goal was something that I could never have even contemplated 12 months ago.

To see my name in the paper the day it was announced was another great moment, but the real buzz came when we got off the coach at the stadium before the match, walked up the stairs and into the dressing room. I had a quick look around and there it was - my very own peg, with my name plaque above it. The last time I had something like that was when my mother was hanging up my coat at nursery school! But there was nothing childish about this. This was it, the toughest assignment of my sporting life and there was no turning back.

The game went quite quickly although I can remember one 50 yard run - well, ok then, five yards!

Then it was the aftermath, a few drinks and the moment I had always dreamed of, walking up to get my cap. I always wondered whether you actually get presented with a cap or whether it would be sent through the post. Well, after the game I was put out of my misery. Martyn Williams got a special presentation for winning his 50th cap and then it was my turn. I was so proud, walking up to shake hands with the WRU president Keith Rowlands. It was the end result of many years of hard work and already I wanted more.

JOHN YAPP

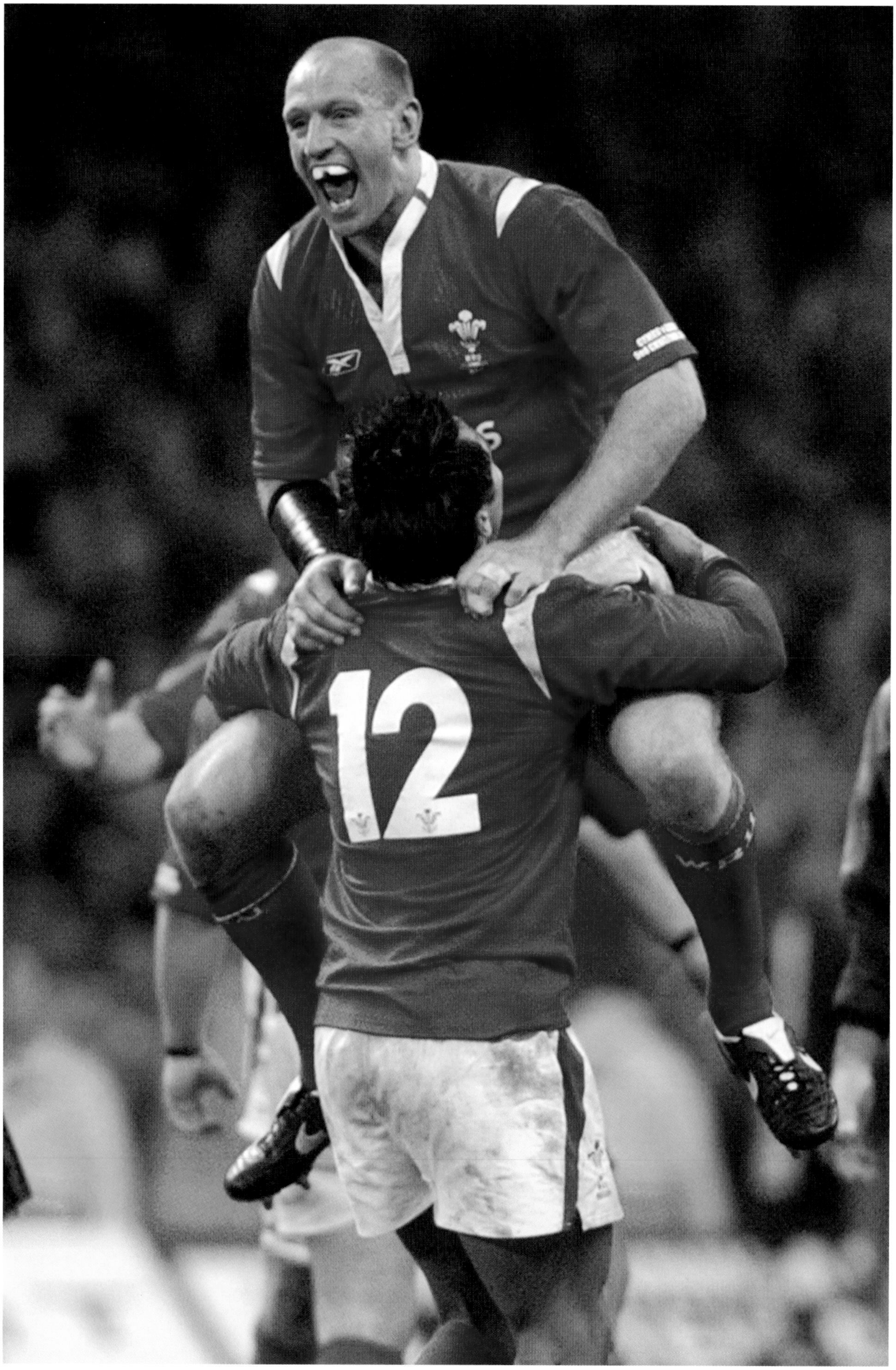
12

Happiness is... beating England at the Millennium Stadium

So much hurt...
now the joy for
Robert Sidoli

Just the beginning: Mike Ruddock addresses the boys to make sure it is the first win and not the last

Clive Griffiths talks tactics with Gav as
Alfie (*right*) gets the party started!

Heroes all!

Referee Steve Walsh can finally see the way forward after sportingly
receiving Alfie's post-match gift before the skipper hands over to
England's Jason Robinson

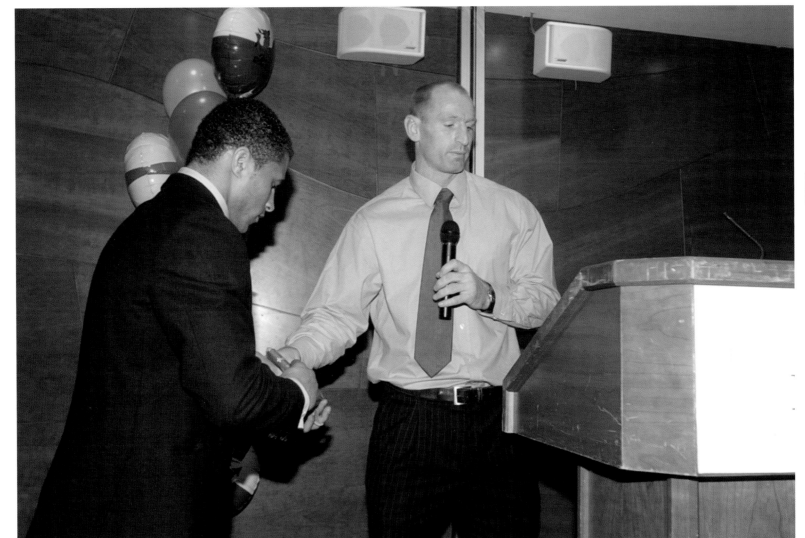

Wales 11   England 9

Wales	England
Gareth Thomas (capt)	Jason Robinson (capt)
Hal Luscombe (Kevin Morgan 68)	Mark Cueto
Tom Shanklin	Mathew Tait (Olly Barkley 62)
Gavin Henson	Jamie Noon
Shane Williams	Josh Lewsey
Stephen Jones	Charlie Hodgson
Dwayne Peel (Gareth Cooper 63)	Matt Dawson (Harry Ellis 67)
Gethin Jenkins	Graham Rowntree (Phil Vickery 59)
Mefin Davies	Steve Thompson
Adam Jones (John Yapp 70)	Julian White (Graham Rowntree 78)
Brent Cockbain (Jonathan Thomas 79)	Danny Grewcock (Steve Borthwick 71)
Robert Sidoli	Ben Kay
Dafydd Jones (Ryan Jones 66)	Chris Jones
Martyn Williams	Andy Hazell
Michael Owen	Joe Worsley (James Forrester 42-44)

Try: S Williams

Pens: S Jones, Henson   **Pens:** Hodgson 3

Sin-bin: G Thomas (38)   **Sin-bin:** Grewcock (38)

Referee: Steve Walsh (New Zealand)
Attendance: 72,500

country	P	W	D	L	for	against	tries	points
Ireland	1	1	0	0	28	17	3	2
France	1	1	0	0	16	9	1	2
Wales	1	1	0	0	11	9	1	2
England	1	0	0	1	9	11	0	0
Scotland	1	0	0	1	9	16	0	0
Italy	1	0	0	1	17	28	1	0

italy v wales

saturday, 12th february, 2005

If Tosh could see me now... Adam
Jones dreams of another career

Ring leaders: Morgan, Cooper and Pugh make a
late bid for Olympic selection

For my next trick: Llewellyn, Williams and Thomas get ready to face the Italians

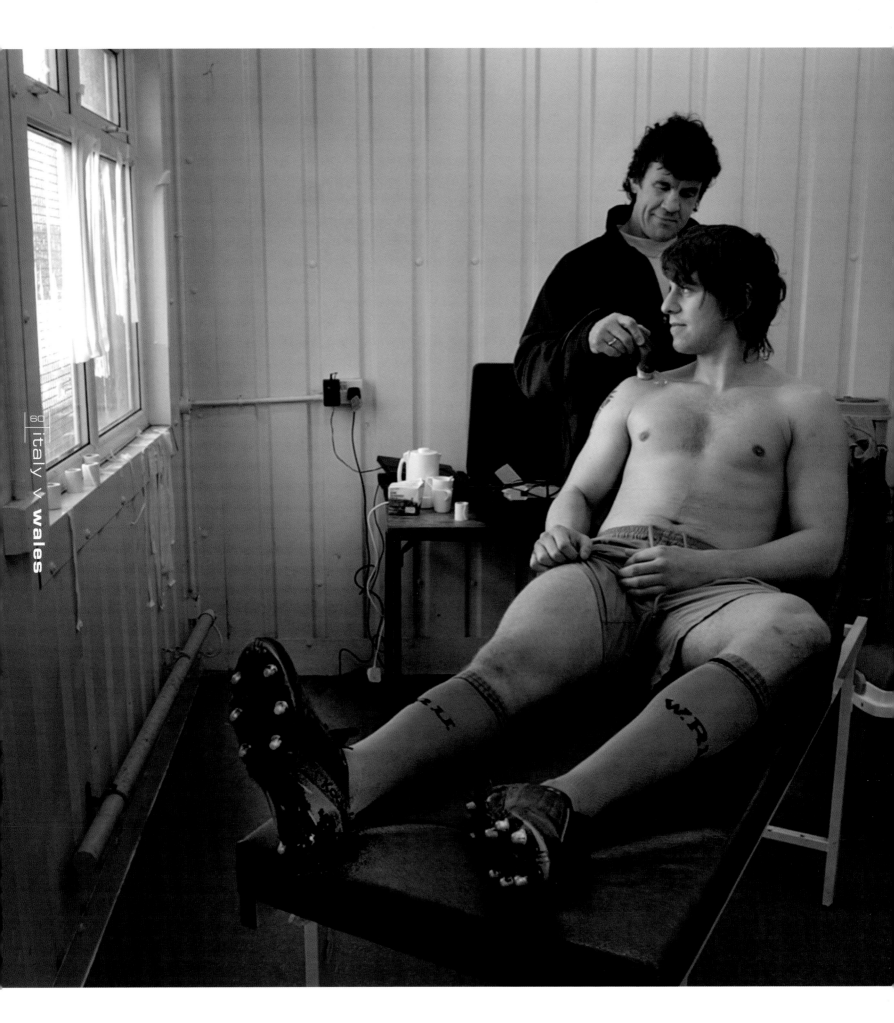

Ryan Jones (*left*) tries out the facilities at the Mark Davies Spa, while Brent, Dafydd and the boss take a breather

DVDs, books and, er, sleeping, provide the on-board entertainment on the flight to Rome

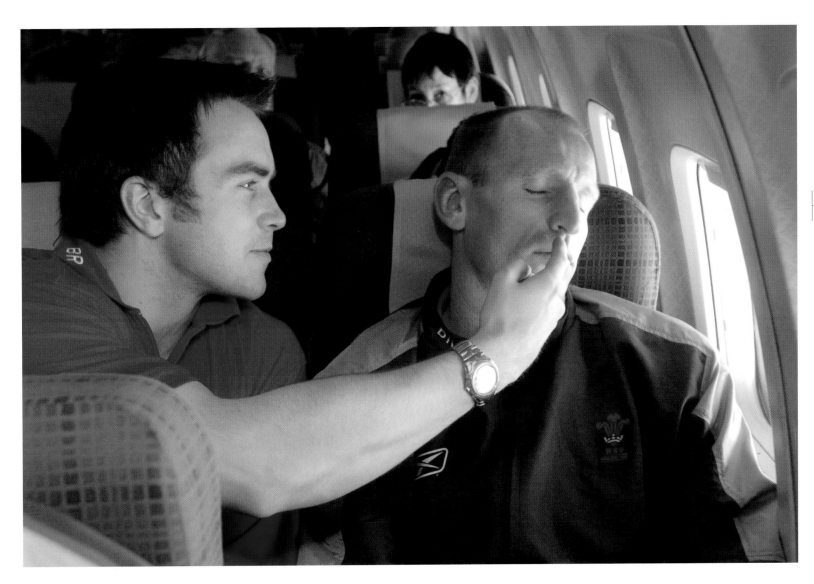

Alfie thinks he's getting some peace until Mr Williams tries a new way to prevent snoring

66

All stand together

Charge! Adam Jones
hits the gap

Jonathan Thomas and
Tom Shanklin swoop
for first half tries

Brent Cockbain powers over the line to score his first ever try for Wales

I n September 2004, Brent Cockbain's baby son Toby Lloyd died from a brain tumour. Since then Brent and his wife Kate have set up the Toby Lloyd Cockbain Foundation, raising thousands of pounds for cancer charities. At a fundraising dinner held between the France and Scotland games during the 2005 Six Nations, Gavin Henson's England match-winning silver boots were auctioned, raising an incredible £8,500.

It's at times like these when you honestly find out who your friends are. Without exception I can say that every single player in this Welsh squad and each member of the team management is as close an ally as you could ever hope to have. On top of that, I also want to send a heartfelt thankyou to each and every Welsh man and woman who has given their time, effort and energy to support myself and my family. It's very touching.

The boys have been fantastic, right behind me 100 per cent. Any time that I have needed anything - whether that be a word of advice or a shirt signed - they have never complained. They put up their hands to do the job and I will be eternally grateful to them for that. I would go as far as saying that it's a tribute to the boys how much money we have raised for charity over the past few months. That support is what makes this squad so enjoyable to be with and, in my view, is the one reason why we have been so successful.

The best way I can describe the camaraderie between the boys is when we turn up for lunch. I have been in squads and teams where you look around the room to see who you can sit next to. Whenever I go into the lunch room, I just grab the first chair. They are all fantastic blokes and they all have their own way of keeping a smile on your face. There is certainly a special feeling at the moment.

I can imagine that the supporters have felt something like that too. Whenever they travel with us, there is always a great feeling between the different groups of fans - it doesn't seem to matter whether they come from Ponty or Cardiff, Swansea or Newport; they are all there together enjoying the laugh and hopefully enjoying the way we play the game.

The fact that we are on a roll has certainly helped and I know the boys are indebted to the fantastic support - from everyone. It has been like that ever since I came to Wales. I have never had a bad word said so I have really enjoyed it.

I think the supporters felt that atmosphere and genuine feeling when we stayed out on the pitch in Rome to celebrate with them. For me it was a great day because it was a great win and I scored my first try. But more than that, it was a good team performance and it was nice to see the donkeys getting four of the six tries.

There will always be a special place for that try and I will never forget walking around the perimeter of the field and seeing so many happy faces. When we got back to the dressing room, we honestly felt that we could go on from there and makes those smiles even wider.

It was probably a defining moment - especially after what had happened in Rome two years earlier.

Dancing feet: Shane Williams squeezes through the eye of a needle to score another sensational try

Can't stop me now... Sidoli is over in the country of his ancestry

My try against Italy in Rome will always be special to me. My father Primo comes from Italy and my brother Peter and myself were on the verge of moving out there two years ago after a significant offer for the two of us was placed on the table. It was a massive offer and very tempting as I'm sure you can imagine. However, we had just finished university over here and after a long discussion we decided to stay put and give it a crack in Wales.

My Dad emigrated from Italy to Cardiff with his brothers, sisters and cousins when he was 18 and they all started work in the café business. He met my mother, who is a Cardiff girl, so that's why I'm half Italian and half Welsh. In rugby terms I'm pretty glad that I chose Wales ahead of Italy right now. I think my Dad is too. Well, at least he told me this season that he has started to support Wales because he has lived here so long! He was so chuffed when we beat Ireland, I think he was more pleased than me - if that's possible.

What makes this incredible Grand Slam all the more special for me personally is that my season started in dreadful fashion. The Warriors had folded at the end of the previous season and I had undergone surgery to solve a long-standing problem with my groin. By the time the autumn series of games came around, I was still struggling for fitness.

Because of that it came as a massive surprise when I was asked along to training with the national squad. Just being around the squad gave me some much needed confidence and after that I just knuckled down to some hard work with my new region, the Blues, and the rest, as they say, is history.

I was picked for the England game which was particularly pleasing because Mike could not have been criticised had he have stuck with his tried and tested combinations from the autumn matches against South Africa and Australia. And from that moment on we've been living in dreamland. I am fortunate to have played in all five games and to cap it all off with that, ahem, 70 metre dash against the Italians...

The result in Rome meant so much. Firstly, it was our first away trip of the campaign so to gain a victory away from Cardiff put us on track. Secondly, and more importantly, victory had a great deal of meaning for all of us who had let our country down in 2003.

Blood, sweat and laughter from Kevin Morgan

There's no hiding place these days as the guys found out the day after the England game. There we were, understandably ecstatic after beating the old enemy for the first time in six years, a squad with plenty to shout about. Or so we thought. Enter Mike Ruddock, his assistants and the video evidence of the game. Victory it might have been, but the camera never lies and in truth we were far from impressive.

Eighty painstaking minutes of analytical work later - and a few raised voices to boot - we realised that unless we knuckled down to some hard work in the week building up to the Italian game, we would probably spend much of the post match reception listening to our captain's speech of apology - just like two years ago.

Little did I know at that stage that myself and five others would actually miss the after-match function in Rome due to sore heads, cricked backs and a variety of cuts, bumps and bruises. Instead of tasting the cheese and wine, we spent our evening under doctor's orders with a cup of coffee and a good book.

Anyway, back to the video nasty. We knew there had been an element of good fortune in the victory over England, if only because we didn't perform anywhere near to our potential. But the tape proved to us that we needed to step up. For me it was a little disappointing to have missed three kicks and in the end I handed the ball to Gav who, thank goodness, did the business.

I'm not one to beat myself up about such a poor return - far from it. However, I was really cheesed off because having kicked so well for Clermont in the build up to the game, I then went and blew it. It was a poor choice of occasion to have a bad day at the office!

So, Monday came, the video had been digested and we were just a few days from a trip to Rome where most of us perished two years earlier. The press and media were still on top of the England game, claiming that miracles had been achieved. They also suggested that we were bang on course for something special. But to be honest, at that stage none of us within the squad had any intention of glancing any further than the impending game at Stadio Flaminio.

Because of that, we were quite calm when it came to kick off and I think that was highlighted in the way we played. We controlled the game and scored a clutch of special tries that gave an indication of what might be ahead. As the game wore on, we became more secure and I was looking forward to seeing out the game and chalking off another challenge. Then, whack, something hit me. It felt like a train at the time, but I think it was a stray, 19 stone Italian forward. Suitably dazed and possibly shell-shocked by that incredible try from Shane Williams, I knew that I would be doing my nation an injustice if I remained on the field. It was no time to be a hero, so I signalled to the bench and the substitution was made.

We won the game with room to spare and although I was still feeling a bit dodgy, I remember a lot of the boys going back on to the pitch to celebrate with the crowd.

For me, Kevin Morgan and the others it was back to the team hotel where the doc and his medical staff kept an eye on us until it was time for bed. There were no dreams that night, just a couple of painkillers and a good kip.

(*left*) So great to see so many of Alfie's family made the trip to Rome!

"Right, what's the Italian for beer?"

So, that's how he lost his teeth

italy v **wales**

BROTHERS IN ARMS
T18
STEPHEN
JONES
WELSH CAP No 956

Calm after the storm:

Gav contemplates

victory number two

Roman conquerors

Italy 8 | Wales 38

Italy	Wales
Roland de Marigny (Matteo Barbini 81)	Gareth Thomas (capt)
Mirco Bergamasco (Kaine Robertson 57)	Hal Luscombe (Kevin Morgan 57)
Walter Pozzebon	Tom Shanklin
Andrea Masi (Matteo Barbini 24-27)	Gavin Henson
Ludovico Nitoglia	Shane Williams
Luciano Orquera	Stephen Jones (Ceri Sweeney 64)
Alessandro Troncon (Paul Griffen 62)	Dwayne Peel (Gareth Cooper 61)
Andrea Lo Cicero	Gethin Jenkins
Fabio Ongaro (Giorgio Intoppa 73)	Mefin Davies (Robin McBryde 66)
Leandro Castrogiovanni (Carlo Del Fava 62)	Adam Jones (John Yapp 66)
Santiago Dellape (Salvatore Perugini 62)	Brent Cockbain (Ian Gough 66)
Marco Bortolami (capt)	Robert Sidoli
Aaron Persico	Jonathan Thomas
Mauro Bergamasco (David Dal Maso 26)	Martyn Williams (Robin Sowden-Taylor 81)
Sergio Parisse	Michael Owen

Try: Orquera

Pen: de Marigny

Tries: J Thomas, Shanklin, M Williams
Cockbain, S Williams, Sidoli

Cons: S Jones 4

Referee: Andrew Cole (Australia)
Attendance: 25,659

country	P	W	D	L	for	against	tries	points
Ireland	2	2	0	0	68	30	8	4
Wales	2	2	0	0	49	17	7	4
France	2	2	0	0	34	26	1	4
England	2	0	0	2	26	29	2	0
Scotland	2	0	0	2	22	56	2	0
Italy	2	0	0	2	25	66	2	0

france v wales

saturday, 26th february, 2005

"You are never going to make that spikey!" Gav offers some grooming advice to Alfie

Reach for the stars:

Jones, Williams, Thomas and

Henson are on the way up

Go on Boys:

One young fan

meets his heroes

france v wales

Cardiff Airport:

Oh the glamour of
international rugby

Five rugby players hanging on the wall

Adam Jones (*left*) in serene contemplation while the boss checks his texts

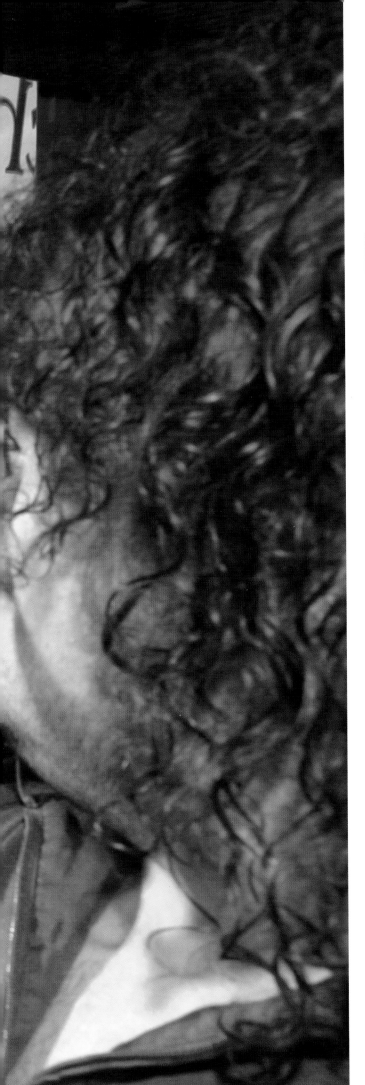

Sightseers: The team (and mascot Taffy!) take in the views of Paris

Don't give up the day job: Alfie

takes the wheel

Cooper tries to break out while Henson (*right*) climbs the stairway to heaven at the Stade de France

Ooh la la!: The French motorcycle police know a fine scrum-half when they see one

Brent Cockbain tapes
up while Rhys Williams,
Tom Shanklin and
Shane Williams decide
the book needs
spicing up!

Holding on: Stephen Jones keeps Wales hanging on in there as France dominate the first half

Comeback king: Martyn Williams was the two-try hero on a famous day for Wales

Foot on the gas: France's Rougerie doesn't even get close to the awesome Shane Williams

Dwayne Peel forces his way through the France defence

wouldn't count myself as one of the more fortunate players when it comes to injuries, but I would certainly count myself pretty fortunate to have played in the defeat of France in Paris.

Okay, so I finished the game with a rather large egg on my head and with the doctors telling me that a night out in Paris was not what they would prescribe after taking such a whack. But when the pain faded away at breakfast on Sunday morning and I was able to reflect on another great win with the boys, of course it was more than worthwhile.

You've got to remember that this time last year I was just about to be made redundant, so as you can imagine the past 12 months has been something of a turnaround. First it was the Warriors going, then a two week spell on the dole as I faced up to the possibility of not getting another region, and now, after some hard work with the Dragons and maybe a little good fortune, I am sitting here with a Championship medal, a Triple Crown and a Grand Slam.

Personally this Six Nations has been a success because I feel as though I have made a contribution - especially in Scotland and against Ireland with the tries.

However, it was more than that in Italy and especially Paris. The try Shane scored in Italy was a team effort where I was able to play a part, and the rearguard action and attacking play we showed in the second half against the French meant I was never far from the action.

We could quite easily have lost in Paris because that first half performance was pretty poor. We lost our way from the first whistle and were lucky that half time came when it did. Obviously Gareth's broken thumb didn't help, but I think his absence in the second half at least proved that we do have strength in depth in Wales. That's not something we have always said about ourselves.

Personally, I was just really pleased for my old Ponty friend Martyn Williams. He has not always been given the opportunity to show how good he actually is. But on this occasion he certainly did. Just look at his contribution in that second half. Two tries, God knows how many tackles and he was always there to support the ball carrier when we turned things around. I have spent a long time playing with Martyn and I cannot think of too many better in terms of a genuine openside. The French game belonged to him.

So what about my bump? Well, I did my best to tackle the full-back Laharrague and although I managed to stop him, I did take a fair crack on the forehead and for a few minutes I felt a little dazed. The Stade de France is a pretty difficult place in which to play, even when you are fully fit. To try and go on when you have just had your head almost knocked off your neck, is even tougher.

Still, I have survived to tell the story and I'm just glad that I was able to play some part in what was probably the most crucial victory of the season. The Scotland game was always likely to be a banana skin, but the French game was always the toughest on paper, regardless of how they were playing at the time.

KEVIN MORGAN

The tension is
unbearable in the last
few minutes

And then the joy is
etched on the face
of Gethin Jenkins

It will hardly come as a great surprise to anyone who knows me, but as a young lad growing up in the Welsh valleys near Pontypridd I longed to play for and captain my country.

To win a first cap, therefore, was the realisation of a dream. To lead my country - for 10 minutes against England, a half against France and then for the whole game against Scotland and Ireland, well... what can I say.

Obviously, I would rather have taken possession of the armband in different circumstances, but such was the position we found ourselves in France that I had precious little time to think about anything else.

I remember my speech to the boys as we left for the field in Paris for the second half. I just turned around and said, "Keep the ball". I'm not sure what they thought about their new captain's 'inspirational' words, but I didn't have a lot else to say. That was it in a nutshell. We had given the ball away in the first half like never before and to be honest we were fortunate not to be a lot further behind.

Mike and the other coaches had said the same kind of thing to us and we knew that if we could keep hold of possession and starve them of ball for a while, we had a chance. And that's exactly what we went out and did.

We kept the ball and our composure and, despite a few frayed nerves and a couple of desperate scrums, at the end, we took the points.

I will never forget that final whistle. The Stade de France is an awesome place to play, and when Stephen [Jones] kicked the ball into touch and the ref blew up, I looked to the skies and realised what we had achieved. If anything the initial feeling was one of relief. We had given it everything and even celebrating was out of the question at that stage.

Having said that, we felt the fans deserved something back from us and we decided to do a lap of honour. It was well worth it because everywhere we looked it was like a sea of red.

The night itself was a bit different. After a few tips from Rupert Moon and a few 'good luck' pats on the back from the boys, I gave my first speech at the post-match meal. The nerves were just as frayed as they had been in the final 10 minutes of the game, but thankfully I got through it and then joined the boys in a celebratory drink.

Now, for those who think we go mad after a game and end up in a bit of right royal mess, you're wrong. Yes, we have a beer or a few glasses of wine, but when we woke up in the morning it was our bodies that were aching - not our heads.

It was a day to remember for me and for all of us - one I know I will never forget.

MICHAEL OWEN

Through the pain barrier: Even a broken thumb can't stop Alfie celebrating with the fans

france v wales

Wow! The boys are too

knackered to celebrate

france v wales

The win and what
these players
have achieved
starts to sink in

Suited and Booted:

The boys smarten up

for a party, Paris-style

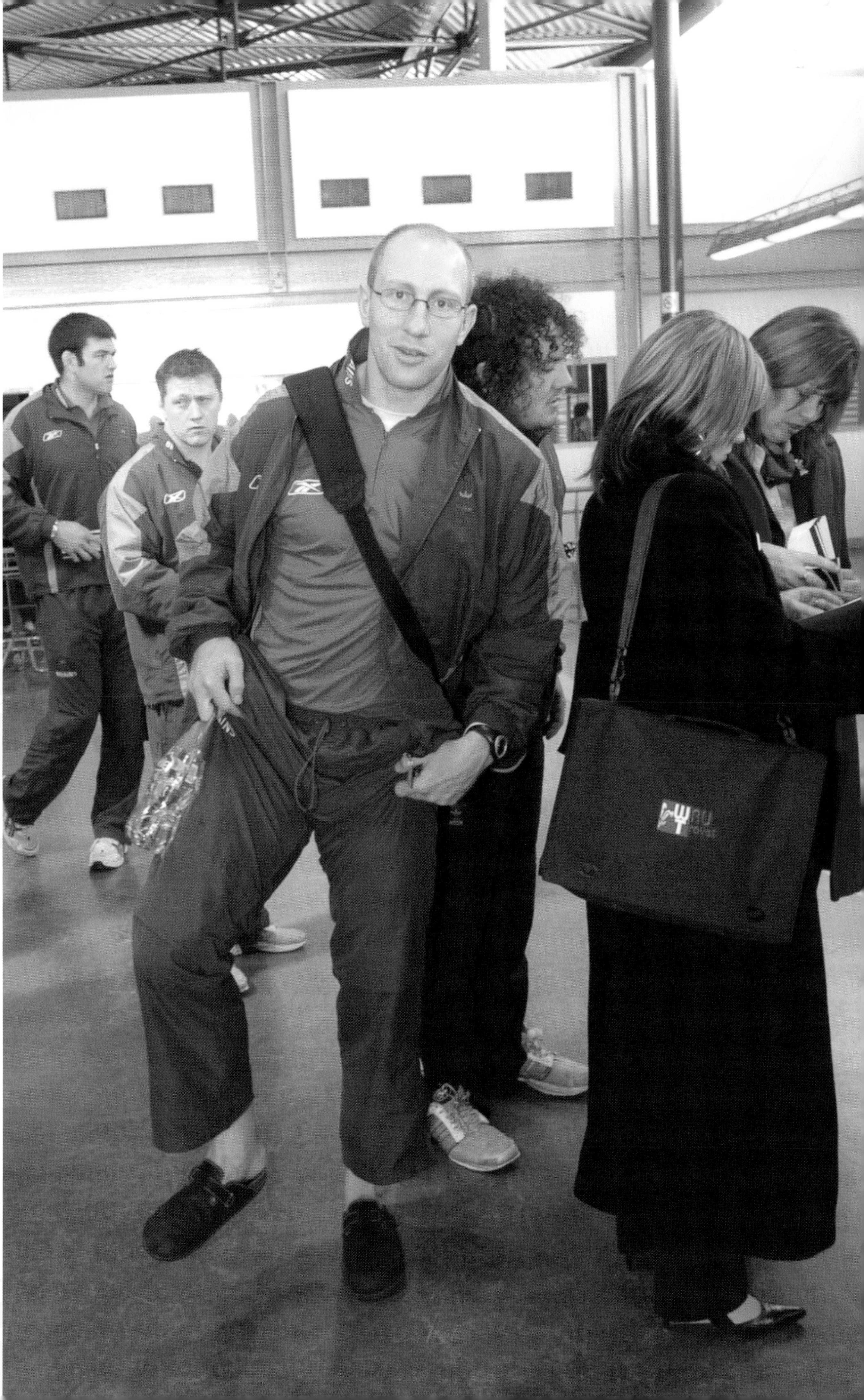

Still going strong
at the airport (*left*),
Tom Shanklin hits
the wall on the
flight home (*pics
courtesy of
Rhys Williams!*)

Tuck in Mefin!

And if there's any
left Ryan will help
you out

France 18 | Wales 24

France	Wales
Julien Laharrague	Gareth Thomas (capt, Rhys Williams ht)
Aurélien Rougerie	Kevin Morgan (Ceri Sweeney 53-61)
Yannick Jauzion	Tom Shanklin
Damien Traille (Jean-Philippe Grandclaude 47)	Gavin Henson
Christophe Dominici	Shane Williams
Yannick Delaigue (Frédérick Michalak 62)	Stephen Jones
Dimitri Yachvili	Dwayne Peel (Gareth Cooper 79)
Sylvain Marconnet	Gethin Jenkins
Sébastien Bruno (William Servat ht)	Mefin Davies (Robin McBryde 76)
Nicolas Mas (Olivier Milloud 50)	Adam Jones (John Yapp 79)
Fabien Pelous (capt)	Brent Cockbain
Jérôme Thion (Grégory Lamboley 76)	Robert Sidoli
Serge Betsen	Ryan Jones (Jonathan Thomas 81)
Yannick Nyanga	Martyn Williams
Julien Bonnaire (Imanol Harinordoquy 61)	Michael Owen

Tries: Yachvili, Rougerie — **Tries:** M Williams 2

Pen: Yachvili — **Pens:** S Jones 3

Con: Yachvili — **Con:** S Jones

Drop Goal: Michalak — **Drop Goal:** S Jones

Referee: Paul Honiss (New Zealand) **Attendance:** 78,250

country	P	W	D	L	for	against	tries	points
Ireland	3	3	0	0	87	43	9	6
Wales	3	3	0	0	73	35	9	6
France	3	2	0	1	52	50	2	4
Scotland	3	1	0	2	40	66	2	2
England	3	0	0	3	39	48	3	0
Italy	3	0	0	3	35	84	3	0

scotland v wales

sunday, 13th march, 2005

Martyn Williams has a dilemma before training at Pontyclun

Just five more minutes please…

(*overleaf*) **Eyes of the dragon:** Adam Jones gets his head right for Murrayfield

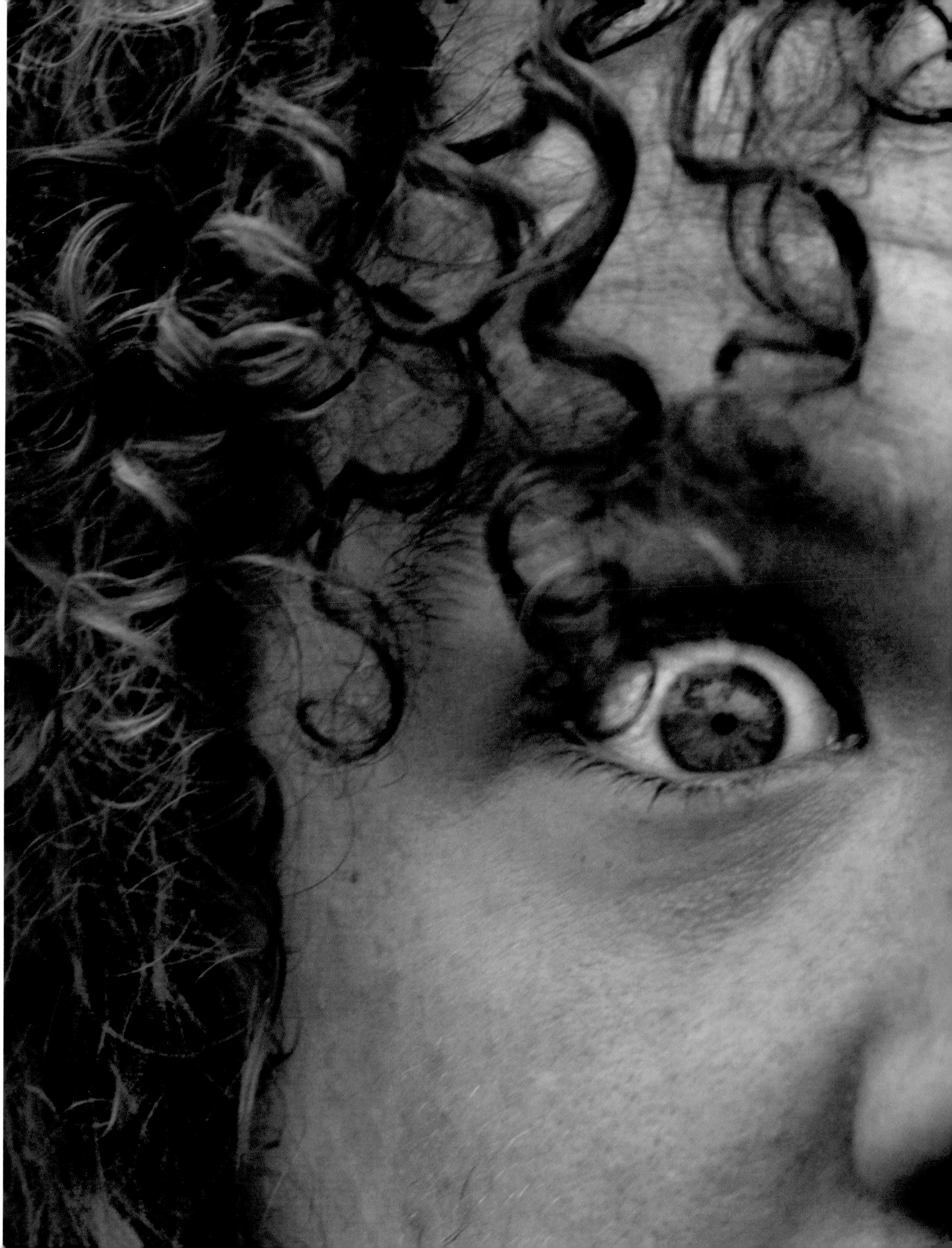

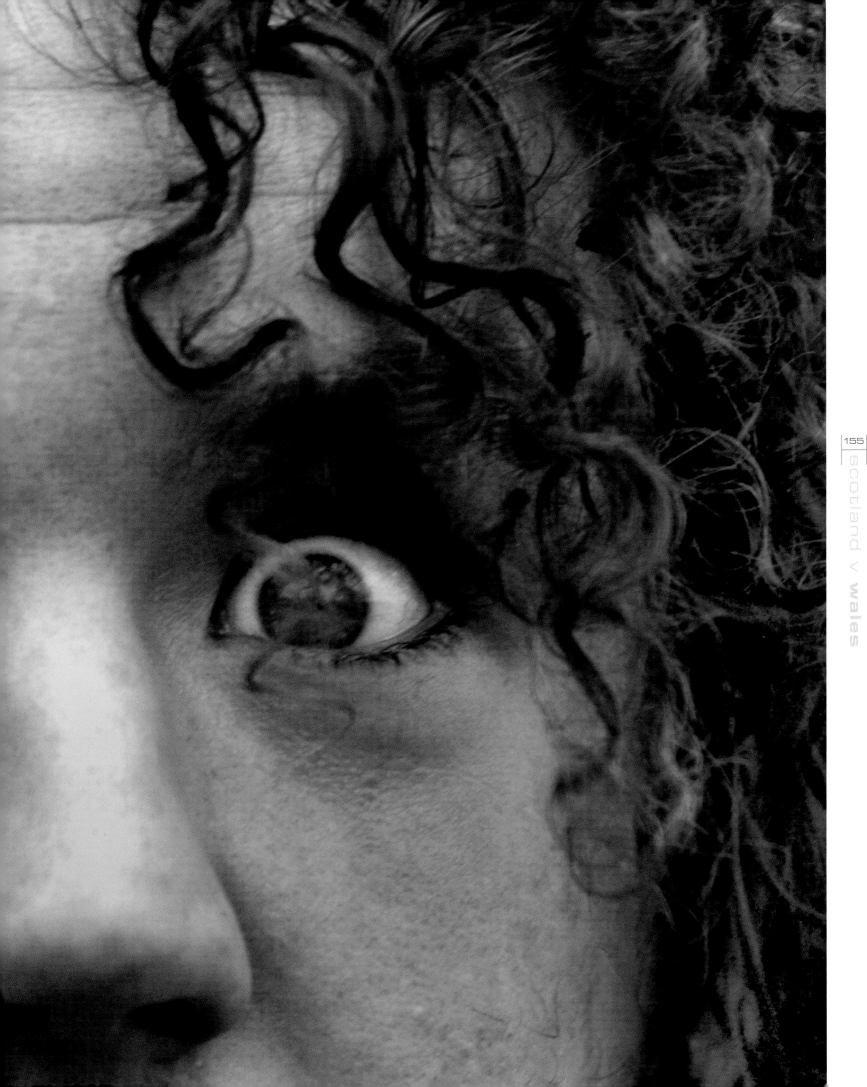

My name is Michael Owen and I'm captain of Wales

John Rowlands has a
special on...15 shirts for
the price of 10

scotland v wales

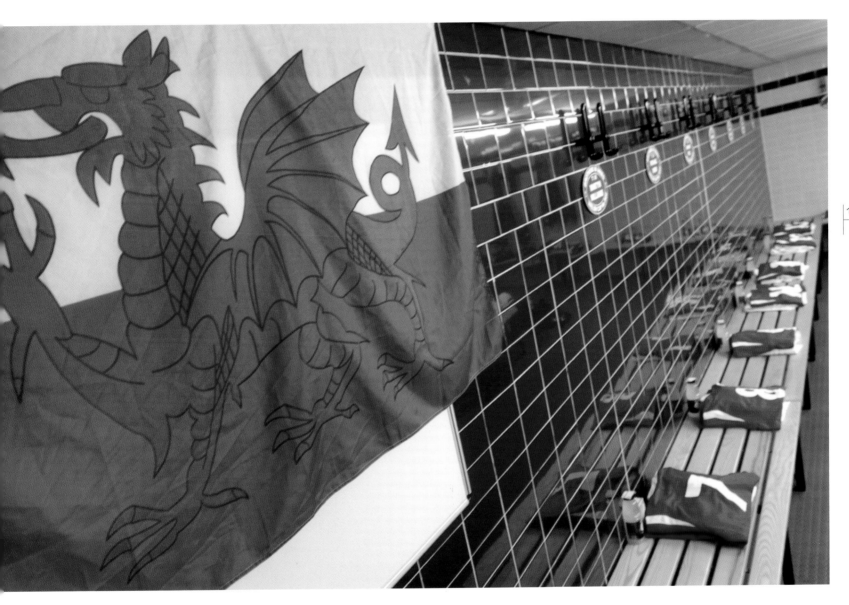

Finishing touches are put to the Murrayfield dressing room

Words of wisdom:

The philosophy that
won a Grand Slam

OUR VALUES

Respect
Unity
Belief
Honesty
Enjoyment
Resilience

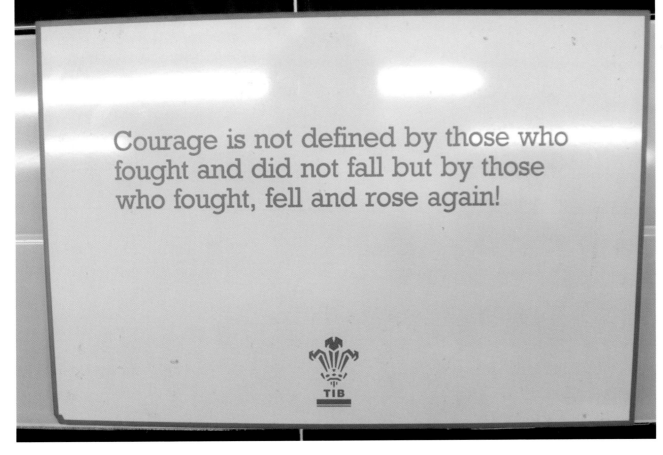

Courage is not defined by those who fought and did not fall but by those who fought, fell and rose again!

(*overleaf*) The 40,000 Welsh fans who travelled to Murrayfield included a bunch of Rhys Williams' mates (*top right*) who all bear an uncanny resemblance to the legendary Scott Johnson.

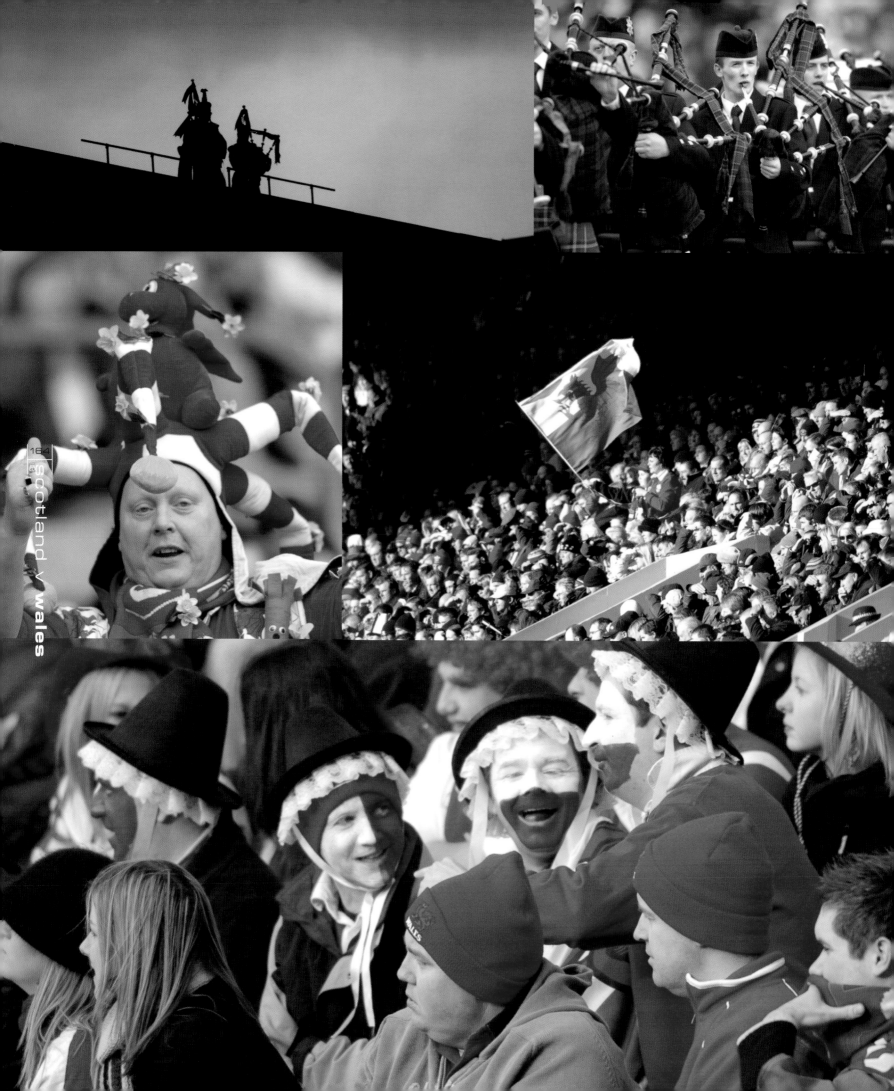

scotland v wales

I spent most of the morning after we beat Scotland having each one of my vertebrae clicked back into place. Aaaargghh!

The pain was even worse than usual. Not because the Scots were any stronger than the French or English, but simply because the game was so quick and we were handling the ball and tackling their players with far greater regularity than usual. I think the ball-in-play time was about 43 minutes - that's six or seven minutes more than normal. So, having sprinted 40 yards to keep up with the boys as we were going forward, we then had to collect ourselves, crouch and engage in a scrum where the hits just got bigger and bigger.

For those who are not quite sure what it feels like when over 100 stone hits you in the scrum, every time it's like, "Oh my God, here we go again!" I looked across at Mef and Adam each time and just said, "come on boys, let's keep going."

Having said that, I would rather be racing around at Murrayfield or Twickenham than working my socks off on the training field - that's when it really hurts. Imagine this. After the French game, we were all aching like hell when we got up on Sunday morning. By the Monday morning things had improved a little and I could actually walk properly. But then, as soon as we got on to the training field, I looked up and saw the dreaded scrummaging machine!

I remember the first set piece. We smashed into the pads and you could hear all eight of our bodies creaking. The pain's immense, but there's no let up. If you want to be the best, or at least mix it with the best, you have to do the hard graft and to be honest all these guys - Mef, Adam, Brent, Sid and the rest - are prepared to put in that graft. No stars, just a bunch of honest boys.

I knew it would be the same after the Scotland game so I went to see Mike, our masseur, who always gets me back in shape, ready for the first session. He lay me down on the bed and gave me a right going over. One by one he went to each vertebra and clicked it back into place. I couldn't believe it was doing me any good, but when I glanced at the paper 10 minutes later and realised what we had achieved at Murrayfield and what might lie ahead, I felt it was a small sacrifice.

Oh, but it gets worse. I woke up a few days later with the first signs of a cauliflower ear. Excuse me for being a bit graphic here, but when the needle went into my ear to drain off all the excess blood, well, that seriously hurt! I gritted my teeth and got through it but felt absolutely gutted when the doc told me that I was now in serious danger of losing my good looks!!!

Anyway, less of the gory stuff. It was a great win at Murrayfield and although we struggled in the second half I have to say that there were plenty of beaming smiles in the dressing room. Even Andrew Hore gave us a smile. I was a little surprised at that because he had spent all of the second half screaming at us and telling us to stop looking at the scoreboard and concentrate on playing the game.

Horey and Scott (Johnson) are fantastic when you're on the field. They really help you focus your minds. When the fatigue sets in - against Scotland I was absolutely knackered after an hour - they just keep on encouraging. Cheers boys, once again it did the trick. Mind you I have to say that in the final 10 minutes of the game I was playing off memory, I was exhausted.

Still, when Horey told us we could look finally look at the scoreboard - after the final whistle, I hasten to add - I must admit to being a trifle chuffed. Four down and one to go.

Now, for another session on the back. Ouch....

GETHIN JENKINS

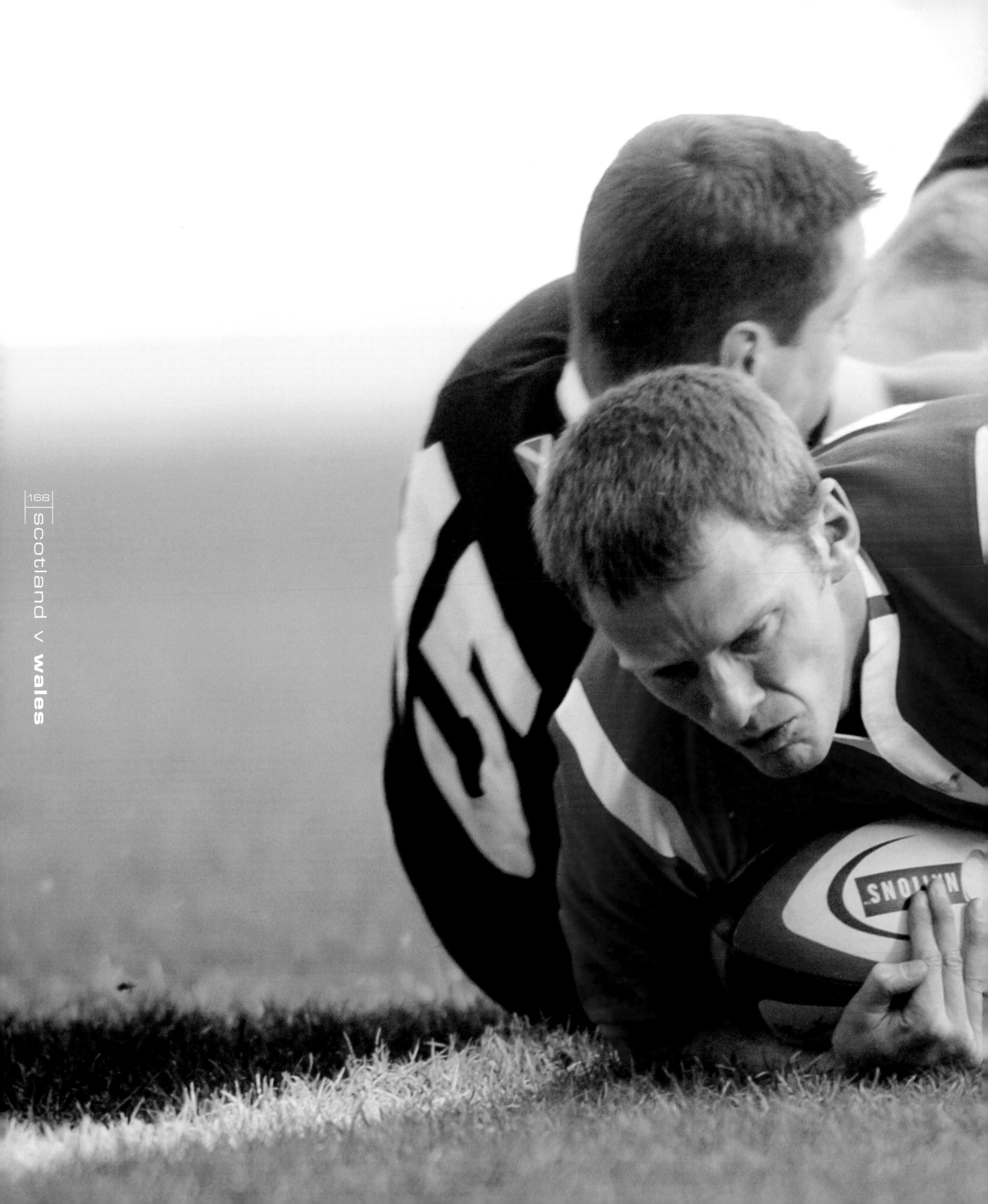

Touchdown: Kevin Morgan goes over on a record-breaking day for Wales

scotland v **wales**

Lift off: Dwayne Peel
sends Gordon
Bulloch flying

Twelve months ago I was regarded by some people as an international rugby player incapable of playing any more than 30 minutes of a Test match. It was not my view but that of others. Thankfully attitudes have changed and under Mike Ruddock, I am now regarded as a player capable of playing 70 or 80 minutes.

Believe me, it's tough enough playing for that long at any level, let alone an international match with so much riding on it.

What's more, when you play in a fast and furious game like we did in Scotland, well, what can I say? My lungs were almost bursting. I'm sure you can understand when I say that a few of us were searching for a second breath within a matter of minutes.

Anyway, having spoken after the game to a few of the Scottish boys, I can tell you one thing, it's far easier when you go 30 points up than it is when you go 30 points down!

Having won in Rome and Paris and having beaten England in Cardiff, we were fully aware of the pressure that was being heaped upon us from those on the outside. We talked about it at length in the build up to Scotland and agreed as a group that this game was the proverbial banana skin.

Seeing as many of us had never been in such a position of strength before, especially not at international level, it was difficult to know how to play it. Should we simply ignore the hype and get on with things, or should we accept that the Scots would come at us in a desperate bid to derail our Grand Slam bid. In the end, we decided to treat it like any other game, concentrate on our own performance and let things happen naturally.

None of us could have expected the game to unfold like it did, but we were delighted to have an opportunity to show exactly what we were capable of producing. We had talked about and practiced that style of play, but on the international stage it's very rare that it comes off with such ease. I thought the boys were fantastic.

As a front row, we worked well. The scrum was fine and in the end, and despite a poor second half, we won quite comfortably and set our sights on Ireland.

It was from that moment that everything happened really quickly. The post-match buffet and speeches gave way to a short coach journey to the airport and a 45-minute flight back to Cardiff. We collected our bags, jumped on the bus back to the Vale of Glamorgan Hotel and headed off to bed without so much as a nightcap.

We were certainly heading in the right direction, but with so little time to prepare for the Ireland game, there was no time for celebration.

We were up at the crack of dawn on Monday morning, into recovery and then off to training to make sure that nothing was left to chance.

I'm not sure when and how the fans travelled to Scotland, but I do know that as we limped on to the training field in Cardiff on that Monday, many of the boys were probably still not back from their weekend north of the border. What a life!

Anyway, not to grumble, those fans are worth their weight in gold and the players were eternally grateful to them for transforming Murrayfield into a sea of red.

He's behind you: Dwayne and Rhys prove too hot to handle

The boys contemplate a stunning six-try win and a shot
at the Grand Slam next week

I know we in Wales get a slagging for all our committees and blazers, but when the season began the squad decided we'd organise ourselves into committees to ensure it wasn't just Gavin Henson who had the smart, clean clothes and listened to his own music on the team bus.

Fortunately I found my way onto the fines committee where, along with Gethin Jenkins and Gareth Llewellyn, we took great pleasure in gathering a few quid from the likes of our esteemed leader [Mike Ruddock] for spending the entire season parking his car in the mother and toddler spaces outside our team hotel at the Vale of Glamorgan.

Then there was the laundry committee, in charge of making sure all our training kit got packed up and sent to the right place (and came back!). Oh dear, sorry JT [Jonathan Thomas] but you were a disaster and you and Dwayne, your partner in the launderette, deserved every bit of stick you got. And did we lay it on thick? Oh yes. At one stage I think JT was scared to come on the bus for the fear of getting another slating.

Thirdly, there was the clothing committee. Now, I'm not one to let out secrets, but the original committee was chaired by the one and only Alan Phillips, our team manager. When it came to choosing some new leisurewear from our clothing sponsors Rockport, Alan would have a major say in things. At this juncture I don't want to say much more, except that the dress sense of a 50-something year old ex-hooker did not sit too comfortably with most of the boys.

Finally there was the entertainments committee, a body of would-be pop-stars which included that hip and trendy centre Tom Shanklin, and the king of the swingers Martyn Williams. I think I would be safe in saying that this was the committee which caused the most controversy. After all, every time we got on the bus we would be subjected to THEIR choice of music.

As soon as the dross came on, straight away you would have Gareth Llewellyn throwing his AC/DC LP down the front, hoping the driver had brought his record player with him, followed closely by Gethin and Yappy calling for a spot of Techno mad hardcore rubbish which seems to strike their respective buttons. I'm surprised it didn't lead to a few bouts of on-coach mayhem. Still, Stephen Jones normally came to the rescue by telling the boys to pipe down. The reason why? Well, Steve likes everything you play and whatever is put on, whether it is Dolly Parton, Whitesnake, Judge Dread or the Stereophonics, Jonesey just said, "This is one of my favourites."

Now, back to the fines committee. First on the list is the aforementioned

Mike Ruddock for his illegal car parking. Secondly and perhaps for an even more serious offence is Haldene Luscombe, my fellow Dragon from Newport. As we set off for the airport to go to Scotland, Alan Phillips made the customary check with the boys.

"Has everyone got their passport?"

"Oh, XXXX,!" came this South African cry from the back of the bus.

"Quick stop the bus, turn around and go back."

Hal had left his passport at home. A quick dash along the M4 later, a massive amount of stick and a few jibes suggesting that he isn't the full ticket, and we were at the airport and checking in. Phew!

In this day and age rugby players are pretty big and powerful and that's probably what enables the forwards, at least, to stand out in a crowd. The same cannot be said of our fitness coach Andrew Hore and our nutritionist Dan King. Neither of them are much over 5ft nothing,

so when they get on the bus together the boys are relentless in their out of tune rendition of, "Hi, ho, hi ho, it's off to work we go..."

Horey also had to bear the brunt of the jokes thanks to a crazy caption in the papers after the England game. I'm sure everyone will remember the state of the pitch. Well, at each breakdown Horey would run on and replace the divots, and the caption under the picture of him in the paper the next day said: 'WRU groundsman replacing divots on pitch.' By 9.30 on Monday morning the article and picture had been pinned up in the team-room and Horey had to look at it every time he dared come in.

They love it really, although Dan wasn't too chuffed when I played the practical joke of the season on him. At various times in a season, Dan asks the boys to supply him with a urine sample so he can check out the various levels of sugar or whatever. Having got on with him so well this year, I decided it was time to have a laugh. So instead of popping off to the little boys room, I grabbed a can of apple juice from the bar and filled my jar with a few tablespoonfuls of the tasty liquid. A few days later he called me over after training and said:

"Ceri, you and I need to talk."

I asked him why.

"Well, I don't know how to break this to you, but your sample is off the scale. It's of real concern to me. Something must be done. "

I kept a straight face for a few moments, but then as I saw the fear of a possible drugs test in his eyes I told him the truth.

It was that kind of season, full of laughs, full of pranks and topped up with the most incredible achievement of our lives.

Scotland coach Matt Williams (*top left*) pays a gracious visit to the
Wales dressing room as the victory starts to sink in

(*overleaf*) **Ah that's ice:**
John Yapp slides into
a medicinal ice bath

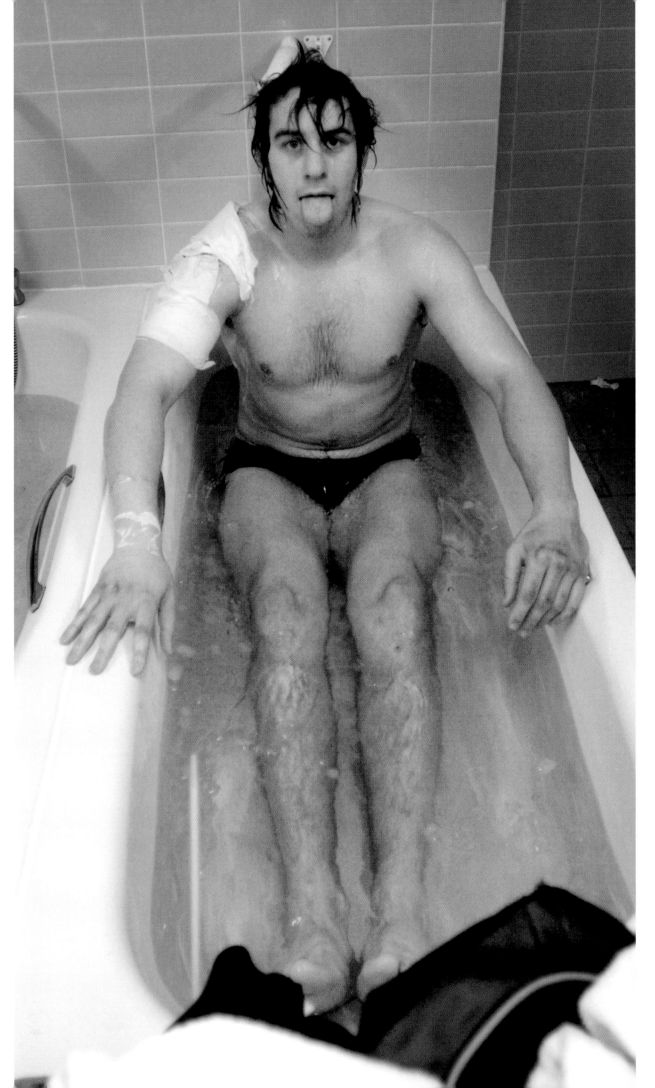

Ryan Jones suffers the
dreaded ice bath while
injured skipper Gareth
Thomas (*far left*) is still
cheering the boys on.

The team is really
starting to gel!

Scotland 22 | Wales 46

Scotland	Wales
Chris Paterson	Kevin Morgan
Rory Lamont	Rhys Williams (Hal Luscombe 72)
Andy Craig (Andrew Henderson 79)	Tom Shanklin (Hal Luscombe 8-16)
Hugo Southwell	Gavin Henson (Ceri Sweeney 79)
Sean Lamont	Shane Williams
Dan Parks (Gordon Ross ht)	Stephen Jones
Chris Cusiter (Mike Blair 50)	Dwayne Peel
Tom Smith	Gethin Jenkins
Gordon Bulloch (capt)	Mefin Davies (Robin McBryde 51)
Gavin Kerr (Bruce Douglas ht)	Adam Jones (John Yapp 66)
Stuart Grimes (Nathan Hines ht)	Brent Cockbain (Jonathan Thomas 74)
Scott Murray	Robert Sidoli
Simon Taylor	Ryan Jones
Jon Petrie	Martyn Williams
Allister Hogg	Michael Owen (capt)

Tries: Craig, R Lamont, Paterson

Cons: Paterson 2

Pen: Paterson

Tries: R Jones, R Williams 2
S Williams, Morgan 2

Cons: S Jones 5

Pens: S Jones 2

Sin-bin: Cockbain (62)

Referee: Jonathan Kaplan (SA)
Attendance: 63,431

country	P	W	D	L	for	against	tries	points
Wales	4	4	0	0	119	57	15	8
Ireland	4	3	0	1	106	69	10	6
France	4	3	0	1	78	69	5	6
England	4	1	0	3	78	55	9	2
Scotland	4	1	0	3	62	112	5	2
Italy	4	0	0	4	42	123	4	0

wales v ireland

saturday, 19th march, 2005

"Ref, did you see that?" Williams is robbed by Shanklin

Mike Ruddock surveys the scene

(right) Stretching out and then pulling together
before the Grand Slam showdown

When Carcass (our physio Mark Davies) asked me how my calf was feeling on the eve of the Ireland game, I just said, "I think we both know, don't we?"

I actually tore the calf about 10 days before the Scotland game and to be honest I was probably not 100 per cent fit when I ran out at Murrayfield on that wonderful Sunday afternoon. Still, when the adrenalin takes over you tend to put up with a little discomfort, especially when it means playing for your country in a game that could leave you one step away from a Grand Slam. I have had my fair share of setbacks in recent years so when the doctor declared me fit I was hardly going to argue was I?

Having said that, imagine what was going through my head when I intercepted Dan Parks' pass inside my own 22 inside the opening 15 minutes. There I was 80 yards from the opposition line, nursing a slight tear in my calf and with 40,000 Welshmen and women urging me on. I set off in pursuit of the posts and I couldn't get there quick enough. At one stage I remember looking around and thinking how happy I was that nobody was on my heels.

The fact that we continued to play so well probably helped me in terms of the injury, and to get another try just after half time (cheers Dwayne) just about crowned the day. In the end, however, I had to give in to the calf and call it a day. I had felt a couple of twinges along the way, but when I bundled Sean Lamont into touch I knew it had gone. I signalled to the bench and hobbled off, pretty disconsolate as you can imagine.

From that moment on, I kind of knew that I would have to miss the Ireland game, although the medical staff worked their socks off to try and cure me. In the end it was not be, although in a way, that was where the fun started. Despite preparing myself for the inevitable failed fitness test, Mike and the staff told me to play it down and make out to everyone else that I would be okay.

When it came to the Friday morning, myself and Mefin pitched up at the Millennium Stadium for our respective fitness tests. We both did a few stretches and Mefin was fine, as we thought. Unfortunately, the moment I stepped up the pace a little, I had to pull up

and raise the white flag.

Once again Mike told me to say nothing to anyone.

"We'll keep it as it is and you can even run out with the boys before the game, as if you're playing," he said.

Mark Taylor was called in to the team with Sonny Parker coming on to the bench. There was a sense of irony about Mark's selection because when I made my debut for Wales back in 2000, it was as a late replacement for Mark. We were rooming together at the time and I remember him turning up at camp on the Monday before the game, having taken a knock in the Swansea v Neath game that weekend. In the end he was ruled out and I got my chance. This time the shoe was on the other foot. He had a word with me on the Saturday and I appreciated that. Mark's a top guy, a great player and a real pro.

Having recovered from the actual disappointment of being ruled out, I took my place on the bus on Saturday afternoon ready for the biggest decoy run of my life. Once at the stadium, Mike told me to grab the number 14 jersey as if I was playing. The plan was simple. I would run out in my kit and warm up with the boys. We didn't want Ireland to have any time at all to prepare for an 11th hour change. Don't get me wrong, Mark is a fantastic player and I think we all saw on the day the full extent of his talent, but Ireland might just have been lifted a little to know that we were scratching around in the dressing room, making late changes in selection.

Once the warm up was over, I slipped off the number 14 jersey, put on my tracksuit and joined the other water carriers.

But the best was still to come. After 20 minutes of the game, Kevin Maggs put in a fairly big hit on Mark and as the two of them peeled themselves off the floor, Kevin said to Mark, "Jesus, when did you come on?"

I had to laugh when Tayles told me, it was brilliant. The plan had worked a treat. On top of that Mark had a great game and played a significant role in another brilliant display from the backs.

Yes, I was still disappointed to have missed it, but just to be there and part of one of the better Six Nations plots in Welsh rugby history was absolutely awesome.

wales v ireland

Pride and Passion: Stephen Jones, Dwayne Peel and Tom Shanklin join Charlotte Church, Max Boyce and Katherine Jenkins for the national anthem

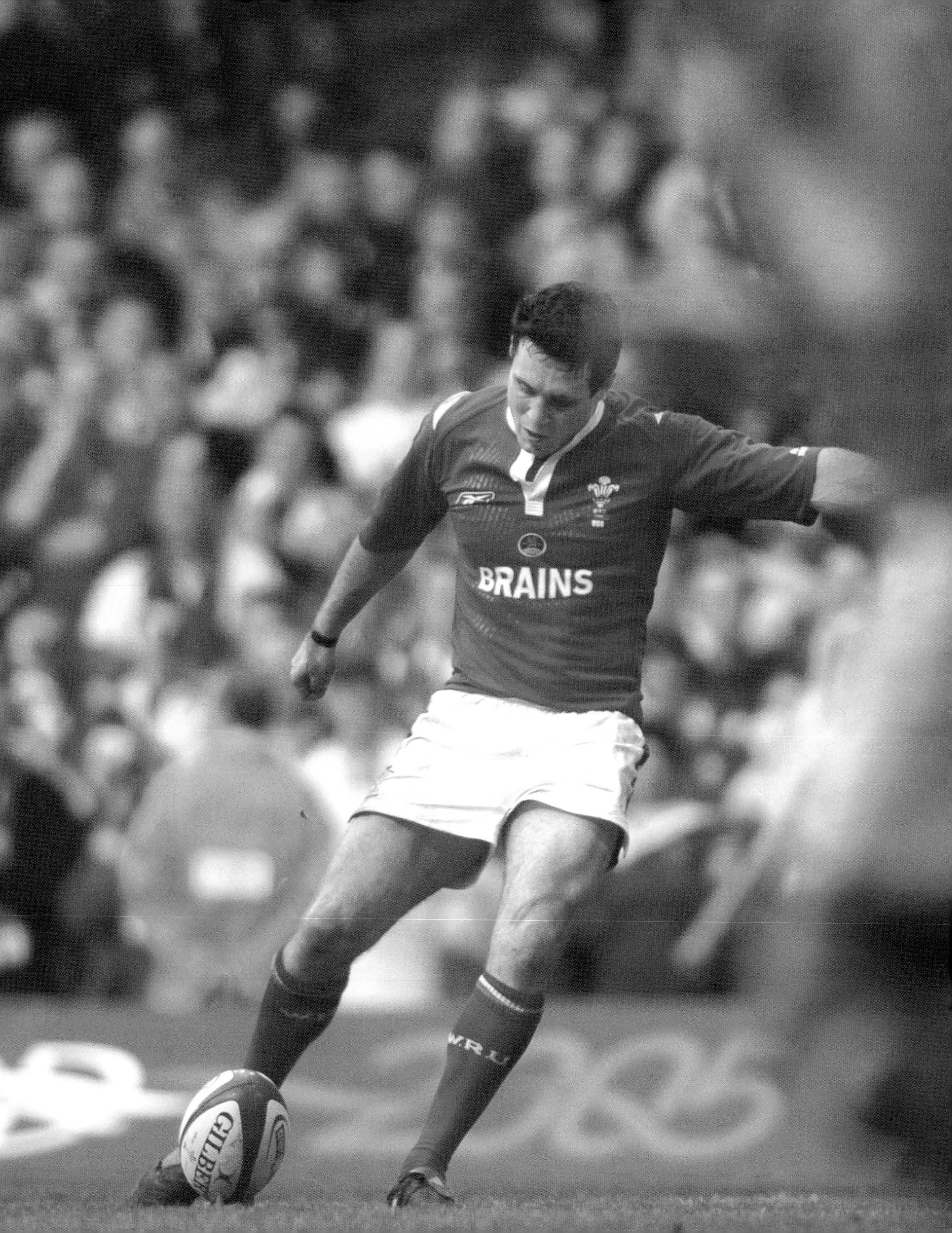
BRAINS
W.R.U
GILBERT

Bootiful: Stephen Jones scored 57 points in the Championship

Get in! Jenkins touches down

Prop Idol

Drop goal heaven for
Henson, and a vital
penalty from inside his
own half follows

Front line troops: The front row
boys prepare to do battle again

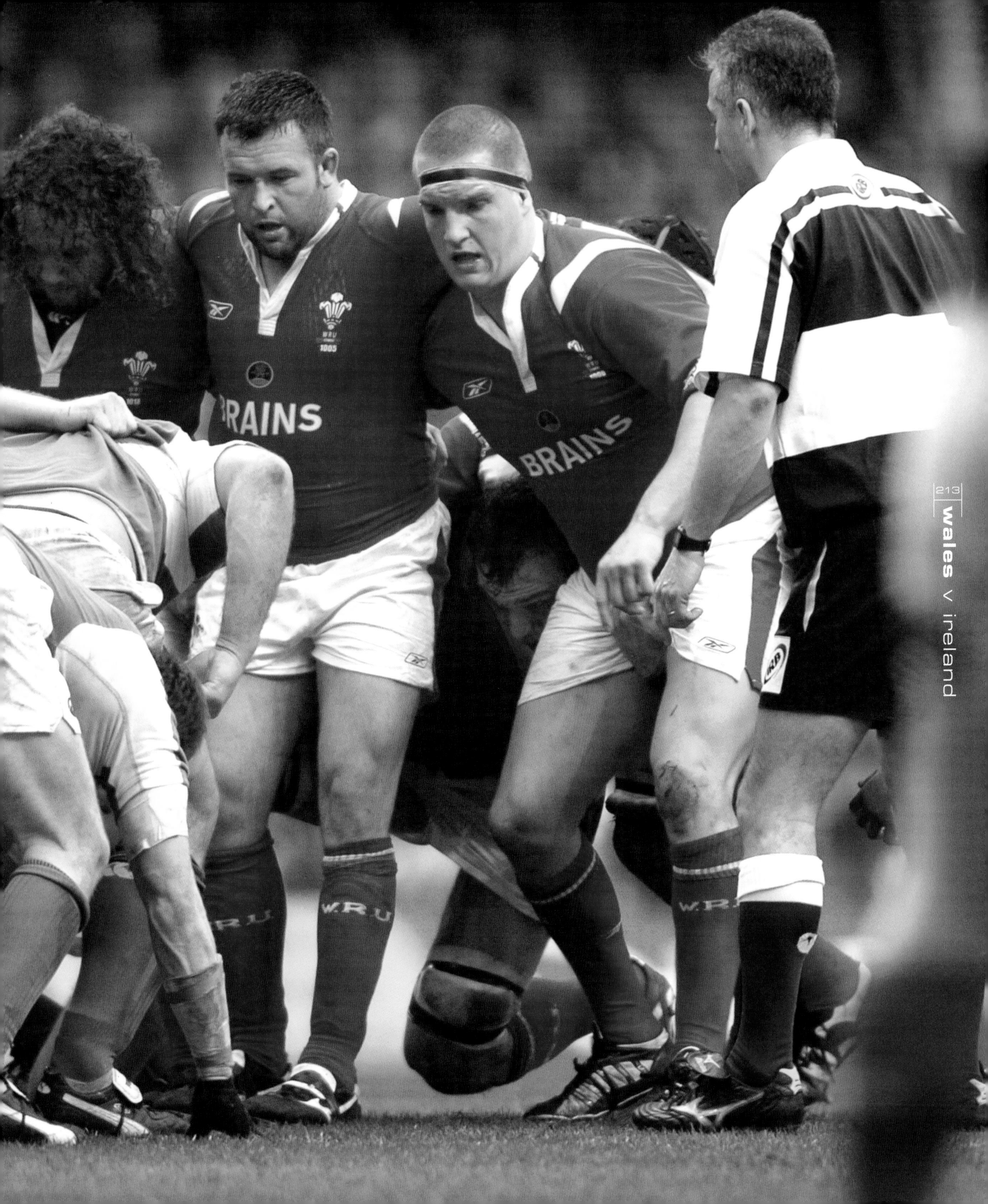
BRAINS
BRAINS
W.R.U.
W.R.U

"Owen to Jones to Shanklin to Morgan... that's the Grand Slam!"

Red hot: Kevin Morgan celebrates the moment the Grand Slam dream became a reality

What a day and what a night... and what a headache come Sunday morning! It has been an incredible journey for all of us, and having arrived at the final hurdle with so much to play for we didn't want to let anyone down - especially when we saw the 250,000 or so people lining the streets of Cardiff as we made our way to the Millennium Stadium.

It started off as a fairly relaxed journey with some of the boys like Martyn Williams listening to their music and the rest of us just sitting there trying to keep cool and thinking of anything but the game. But when we started hitting the outskirts of Cardiff it was difficult to do anything but soak it all up and become heavily involved. They were 10 deep, all the way from Ninian Park, or so it seemed. It was an incredible feeling for all of us.

Personally I have got a lot better in terms of dealing with that pressure. When I first played for Wales I would get really nervous, but as you become more experienced you learn to handle situations. On this occasion it was tougher than ever, but we all knew what was at stake and that if we allowed ourselves to crumble we would end up with nothing to show for our efforts.

Now, as one of the jokers in the pack, I normally have a wise-crack or two to bring some of the superstars down to earth - a little quip here and a clip around the ear there normally does the trick. But on this occasion there was no room for that kind of stuff. The dressing room was relatively quiet. We got changed, warmed up and after listening to an inspirational talk from Michael Owen we decided to get out there and get on with the job.

For me the game was always going to be difficult because of my proximity on the pitch to a certain Brian O'Driscoll. He's a great player and we knew that if he got going and played well we might find ourselves under some real pressure. I'm not going to judge myself, but I think I did okay in that battle.

The one battle that surprised me was the incident involving Paul O'Connell and Sid's head. O'Connell had Sid on the floor and was giving him a few whacks. I remember running over with some of the other boys - just to see how hard those macho forwards fight - and saying to Paul, "Come on Rambo get off him". Peely called the big Irishman 'Ginger' (I think he said it from one and a half arms lengths away, however) and the rest of us were muttering a few things under our breath.

It was so funny but not quite in the same league as Geth (Gethin Jenkins). Whenever Ronan O'Gara kicked the ball, Gethin kept telling him if he carried on being boring and kicking every ball they won, he would end up with a cauliflower foot. It was all good natured stuff and after the game the two sets of boys got on great at the dinner.

For me, well, I was delighted with my own performance and that my two sisters and cousin turned up along with my father. Having said that, I'm not sure whether he saw much of the game. Ever since the day I suffered a really bad thigh injury he's been a little concerned about me playing. As a result he doesn't come that often. On this occasion I can certainly say, 'he was there'. Well, he was in the stadium, but I think the anxiety got a bit much because when he phoned me at the end of the game he admitted he'd spent most of his time walking around the corridors unable to watch.

For us, well, what can I say. It was the most phenomenal day of my rugby career. To sum up an incredible Six Nations what can I say? Simply that I am proud to have been part of his squad and proud to be Welsh. I cannot say any more.

TOM SHANKLIN

On top of the world: Dwayne and Brent

enjoy a moment of history

"We did it!"

Girl power:

The players' families
and friends were a vital
part of the Grand Slam
winning team

Lapping it up: Stephen Jones leads the celebrations and Brent Cockbain
stops to shake hands with the presenters of TV show *Scrum V*

The 2005 Six Nations was an unbelievable experience from start to finish, but I don't think anyone could blame me for feeling a little flat when the dust settled on our Grand Slam success.

I lived every minute of those final two games - against Scotland and Ireland - despite being denied the chance of playing any significant role. But it wasn't quite the same for me. I am not and never have been one of those easily-pleased players who can tag onto someone else's success. Unless I can provide a real contribution to the cause, I tend to feel a little empty. This was the perfect case in mind.

For the opening three games, I honestly felt on top of the world. I was pleased with my own performances and, more importantly, delighted that the side was proving people wrong by sweeping aside the likes of England, Italy and France. I felt as though I had done my bit to help this fantastic squad establish a real foothold at the top of the Six Nations table. Then the injury struck and that was that.

The final two weeks - for me at least - were desperate, although I tried hard to keep a smile on my face whenever I was around the players and the public. I tried not to allow my real feelings to push their way to the surface. Those feelings were reserved for my wife Jemma who helped no end when it got really tough. I don't think anyone out there can imagine the extent of the pain deep inside my gut. On the one hand I was living this Grand Slam dream and on the other I was resigned to a watching and helping role. I was hurting like I have never hurt before.

In the end my charade was so convincing that the whole nation must have thought I was over the initial pain and living the dream along with the rest of the squad. Don't get me wrong, there was nothing false about the smiles of jubilation at the final whistle of the Ireland game, but it was all a little tarnished by the bloody plaster on my hand. Why me?

Still, here we are, 30-plus players, a dozen or so back room staff members and an entire nation with a little piece of history in our pockets. And boy does it feel good to have been part of it. It was an incredible feat and I am proud of every single member of that party for what they have achieved in such a short space of time. It seems like an age since we were suffering at the hands of the big guns and subsequently the press and media. It has been a wonderfully rewarding journey and one which has certainly silenced a few of those cynics who appeared to take great pleasure watching us languish around amongst the dead men in recent seasons.

As a Welshman I feel particularly honoured. As captain I can't speak highly enough of the guys, every one of them. As a fellow player, I knew I could rely upon each and every one of them.

The captaincy part of the story still beggars belief; I still cannot quite comprehend that Mike Ruddock handed me the armband last year. Right from the outset I wanted to captain my country and I made

that quite clear when Mike started to talk to me about the job. I never for one moment thought I would get it, so when the offer came I was shocked. I actually had to think twice about it, such was my surprise. It was not that I was really having second thoughts, far from it. I think it was more that I couldn't quite see myself telling our previous captain, Colin Charvis, and that I couldn't imagine standing up in front of the boys and giving my first speech.

I took the bull by the horns as far as Colin was concerned and he, as you would expect, took it well. He wished me well and in a way that allowed me to move forward and tackle the next task - leading the squad.

Their response has been fantastic, right across the board and I hope that the respect I have for them is felt by them towards me.

Gradually, day by day, we grew together as a squad and in the end we had a spirit running through the camp like I have never witnessed before. When the going got tough, we most certainly got going. We could rely on each other; trust each other; we would do anything for each other - on and off the field.

During my career I have worked and played under some very good leaders. Rob Howley, Scott Gibbs and Scott Quinnell were three of the best captains I have ever met and I suppose, in a way, I have brought elements of their leadership into the way I lead the side. Having said that, when Mike sat me down at the outset to talk about the future, I made it quite clear that I wanted to do things the Gareth Thomas way.

There are two sides to me when it comes to leading the side. Firstly, there's the serious player and captain who ensures that things are done properly on the pitch. Secondly, when the sessions are over and matchday has gone, I let my hair down and actively encourage the other players to follow suit.

When we walk on to the training pitch I expect the highest standards. When we walk off the field, that's it. There is no benefit in putting added pressure on the players by being serious and rigid for 24 hours a day. I like to have a laugh and to make sure that come the weekend the boys are refreshed and desperate to play, not bored and tired of pulling on their boots.

I know next year is a long way off and that I still have to get myself fit to have any chance of playing a part. However, I cannot wait to be back amongst the Welsh boys and proving myself good enough, once again, to succeed on the toughest stage.

However, I still wake up and wish that I could have been there at the end, wearing a jersey and having done my bit for the cause. It wasn't to be, but who knows, next year could be the one for me. Let's hope so.

But for the time being, I am one proud player and captain and thanks to each and every player for the part they player in what has been a magnificent triumph.

GARETH THOMAS

Bubble bath:

Ceri Sweeney cracks
the first of many

W inning Habit
A ggressive
L icence to Thrill
E xcellence
S mile – Enjoy

Stephen Jones polishes his shoes for the post-match party while Gareth Cooper gives the trophy a whirl

236

wales v ireland

The Three Degrees:

Parker, Jones and

Williams heading for

number one

Champions!

239

wales v ireland

Wales 32 | Ireland 20

Wales	Ireland
Kevin Morgan	Geordan Murphy
Mark Taylor	Girvan Dempsey
Tom Shanklin	Brian O'Driscoll (capt)
Gavin Henson	Kevin Maggs
Shane Williams	Denis Hickie
Stephen Jones	Ronan O'Gara (David Humphreys 51)
Dwayne Peel	Peter Stringer
Gethin Jenkins	Reggie Corrigan (Marcus Horan 63)
Mefin Davies (Robin McBryde 72)	Shane Byrne (Frankie Sheahan 66)
Adam Jones (John Yapp 70)	John Hayes
Brent Cockbain	Malcolm O'Kelly (Donnacha O'Callaghan 66)
Robert Sidoli	Paul O'Connell
Ryan Jones	Simon Easterby
Martyn Williams	Jonny O'Connor
Michael Owen (capt)	Anthony Foley (Eric Miller 62)

Tries: Jenkins, Morgan | **Tries:** Horan, Murphy
Cons: S Jones 2 | **Cons:** Humphreys 2
Pens: Henson, S Jones 4 | **Pens:** O'Gara 2
Drop Goal: Henson |

Referee: Chris White (England)
Attendance: 74,000

country	P	W	D	L	for	against	tries	points
Wales	5	5	0	0	151	77	17	10
France	5	4	0	1	134	82	12	8
Ireland	5	3	0	2	126	101	12	6
England	5	2	0	3	121	77	16	4
Scotland	5	1	0	4	84	155	8	2
Italy	5	0	0	5	55	179	5	0

THE DAY OF A LIFETIME...

I woke up this morning about 8.30am and realised it was Judgement Day. Beating England, Italy, France and Scotland had left us all on a real high, but deep down there was a genuine feeling of real anxiety. Just look at the records - Ireland hadn't lost in Cardiff for 22 years, or something like that, and they were obviously smarting from their defeat at home to France.

After going through the everyday ritual of washing and cleaning my teeth and telling my room-mate Ryan Jones to try and calm his nerves, we dressed, met a few of the other guys on the landing and dropped down to the restaurant for a bite to eat.

For breakfast I had my usual pre-match feed, plenty of scrambled egg and bacon and whatever else is going. I'm sure that Dan King (our dietician) must have been up all night measuring the portions, because although I was absolutely starving I was told not to go for the fourth Shreaded Wheat and the seventh sausage but to concentrate on what would keep me in trim for the game. Dan is the man, he's wonderful at his job and although I was a little miffed last summer when I was told to stay away from the tour to Argentina and South Africa in order to bulk up, I have to say that he has played no small role in helping me realise the latest goal in my career.

So, suitably fed and watered (I did pinch an extra spoonful of yoghurt when Dan wasn't watching) I thumbed through The Western Mail and a few other papers to read how the nation was expecting us to achieve what we could only have dreamed of at the beginning of the season.

The papers have been quick to criticise us in the past and to be honest some of it hurt. How times change. Here they were telling us that we were going to win the Grand Slam for the first time in 27 years. If the pressure from within was not enough, it was certainly building on the outside.

Having digested my food I decided to revert to my other match-day ritual of getting away from the guys for just 15 minutes or half an hour to focus my own thoughts.

Our team hotel is pretty remote for home games, a mile or so from the M4 in the Vale of Glamorgan. So, with nothing else on the other side of the perimeter fence but a golf course and a few fields, it's not exactly the ideal location to soak up the pre-match atmosphere - like you can in Dublin or Edinburgh. So, instead of popping into Next or Woolies to see what I might buy the next time I'm in Cardiff, I turned left down the main driveway of the hotel, walked alongside the 18th fairway of the new course and tried to collect my thoughts for a while.

By the time I returned to the foyer of the hotel, you could feel the tension building. There were good luck messages everywhere and the members of staff had big smiles on their faces. They all had their fingers crossed, hoping that we could add the final chapter.

I went back to the room where Ryan was watching a bit of television. Now, Ryan is like Jenks when it comes to match-day. Jenks would always start retching on the morning of a game and would continue to do so until the final few minutes before the game. The tension of the occasion affects some players like that and Ryan is one of them, so I had a little chat to him and assured him that we would be alright.

It's tough on matchday because the game can't come quick enough. I find myself glancing at my watch every five minutes, waiting for the time that we have to get on the bus.

At last it was time to go. I collected my shower bag, black tie and DJ for the party we'd attend - win, lose or draw - and made my way down to the foyer where most of the boys were waiting. The last time I was in the foyer the boys were laughing and joking. Now it was a different story. I looked around and with the exception of Gav and a few others - none of whom suffer from nerves - there were some pretty anxious looking guys. I wanted to sit down and have a chat with someone, but I just bundled my stuff into the boot of the coach and climbed aboard, ready for the 10 mile journey to the stadium.

As one of the members of the entertainment committee, I thought about choosing the music. Well, that was the plan. The reality is that I could hardly move. The nerves had set in and I was really struggling.

The jokers did their bit to break the silence, but this was different. This wasn't any old journey to any old game - this was everyone's day of destiny. The coach pulled away from the front of the hotel and I looked back to see the last few members of staff and a few guests waving us goodbye. There was no turning back.

The mile to the M4 seemed like an overnight excursion. Every yard was like a mile, every minute like an hour. Gradually as we made our way into Cardiff, the crowds grew in number and red shirts could be seen on every corner. We passed Ninian Park and then on into town, over the bridge and into Westgate Street where you could hardly see a square metre of pavement. There were literally tens of thousands of people screaming and waving.

I could hardly prise myself out of my seat as the bus came to a halt under the stadium. One by one, in total silence, the boys filed off the bus and up the steps to the changing room. I think Ireland had already arrived, but to be honest I just had a quick look down the tunnel and then set my eyes straight on the dressing room door.

I have spent some pretty bad afternoons in and around this stadium, and I knew that within a few hours we would either be toasting a job well done or preparing ourselves for another slating in the press.

For those who don't know or have not been on one of the stadium tours, each player has his own changing place with a plaque above it. I always cast a glance at my name, even now. I have never taken anything for granted and I never will. On this occasion I looked up just to confirm that it was me, here, waiting to play in the most important game of my life.

I sat down and grabbed a programme to flick through it, hoping that I might find something to read, just to take my mind off the game itself. Ryan was next to me, retching as usual and providing a timely reminder of the importance of the occasion.

The bandage boys got their dressings done and then, about 45 minutes before the game, we all went out to get warmed up. At that stage of proceedings, the stadium is usually half full with the other half finishing their beers somewhere in town. On this occasion, the ground was almost full. The singing was deafening and the boys could hardly breathe.

About now I started to feel a little better because my boots were on, the shirt was mine and I could let off a little steam. When the warm up was complete, we came back in and had a laugh as Rhys gave his jersey to Mark Taylor.

Michael Owen has done a great job as captain after Alfie was ruled out through injury and he stood up and spoke superbly well. Michael's a man of not too many words, but each word he spoke on this occasion was meaningful and emotional. From that moment I knew that this would have to be our day. There was no point in having come this far just to fail.

The game was incredible in terms of its pace and passion and although we started a little sluggishly, Gethin's chargedown try turned the tide and suddenly the belief came flooding back. Just before half time I collided with someone's boot or knee and all of a sudden on came our physio Mark Davies to inform me that my nose was splattered half way across my face. Well, perhaps that's a bit of an exaggeration but it was quite bloody and quite messy. At that point it would have taken a pack of wild horses pulling another pack of wild horses to get me off that pitch. Mark wiped away the blood gave me a smile and said he would patch me up at half time.

He did that and in the second half, apart from stupidly dropping one pass, I felt fine and even had the pleasure of being the last person to touch the ball before the final whistle. I will never forget it. It was the final minute and I knew that the next stoppage would signal the end of the game. Gethin, once again, secured the ball in our 22 and as it popped out, I picked it up and booted it into row Z, Game over!

The scenes were incredible and I still struggle to find the right vocabulary to describe how we felt as we lapped up the applause and celebrated with the trophy. It must have been 45 minutes before I jumped in the bath and got the old DJ on. One by one we were allowed to invite our immediate families into the dressing room for photos with the cup and then after that we fought our way into the bus and through the crowds and onto the formal dinner at the Hilton. Little did I know that we had more entertainment in store.

From the Hilton we went to the Brains Brewery pub where we continued our celebrations with our friends and families. That particular session went on for a couple of hours until our leader, Mister Mike Ruddock, announced that by chance he had with him his guitar. Ten Elvis songs and a few REM remix versions later we were tripping the light fantastic and rounding off a wonderful day and a wonderful season.

I will never forget this day, or these two months, for as long as I live.

MARTYN WILLIAMS

Suits you, Sirs: Jenkins, Cockbain,
Jones and Sweeney plus trophy
escorts Michael Owen and Robin
McBryde get ready to rumble

The party turned out to be a quiet, laid-back affair!

247 wales v ireland

Gav is caught on the
hop while Sweeney and
Morgan are mobbed

And then things started to get a bit blurry...

With the dust settling after the Grand Slam triumph and with his champagne-sodden suit barely back from the dry cleaners, triumphant coach Mike Ruddock sits back to reflect, player by player, on the squad that has put the pride back into Welsh rugby.

Colin Charvis

The man of the autumn series by some margin, Colin was unlucky to suffer a really nasty ankle injury against the Dragons in the Heineken Cup. However, thankfully he is over that now and can look forward with relish to the summer.

2005 Six Nations: 0 appearances

Brent Cockbain

Brent is a special man who has gone through some difficult times off the field. However, despite that, he always been there as a real key member of the party and the fact that the players all love him to bits speaks volumes. His try against Italy proved what can be achieved with that level of determination.

2005 Six Nations: 5 appearances

Gareth Cooper

A magnificent player who has been so unlucky with injuries this season. Came off the bench to give us real continuity in the opening games but unfortunate to get an injury in the North v South match.

2005 Six Nations: 3 appearances

Mefin Davies

An outstanding performer who got better and better and better as the tournament went on. His mobility and footballing skills were first class and his tight work was excellent. I just cannot understand why he wasn't picked far earlier in his career.

2005 Six Nations: 5 appearances

Ian Gough

Fought his way out of the wilderness and back into the squad with some outstanding performances in the Heineken Cup, most notably against Newcastle. Tough tackling lock who never let us down.

2005 Six Nations: 1 appearance

Gavin Henson

I am pleased with his progress. We brought him in on the summer tour and looked at him as a 12 and then a 15 against the Baa-Baas. I think he is a fine 12, a good playmaker and a fine kicker.

2005 Six Nations: 5 appearances

Gethin Jenkins

There are not enough superlatives to even start talking about this man. England built up Julian White before our first game against England and Gethin destroyed him. After that he was impeccable, not just at the scrum but in his tackling, ball carrying and passing before contact. His charge down try against Ireland simply capped the most incredible personal performance.

2005 Six Nations: 5 appearances

Adam Jones

I am so pleased with Adam. He had a reputation as a 30-minute international before the start of the season, but he has turned that around very, very well. He was very effective in the scrum and never played less than 70 minutes in a match.

2005 Six Nations: 5 appearances

Duncan Jones

Very, very unlucky to get injured in the Heineken Cup against Munster. His broken thumb ruled him our of the first half of the competition and during that time Gethin and John Yapp took their respective opportunities.

2005 Six Nations: 0 appearances

Ryan Jones

I brought in Ryan to give me another ball carrier who could bust tackles. He did that against Scotland and got us on the way by starting and finishing that first try. He can only get better from here.

2005 Six Nations: 4 appearances

Stephen Jones

Just magnificent, from start to finish. We can talk as much as we like about our half-time words of wisdom in Paris, but it was Stephen who turned that match and none of us will ever forget that.

2005 Six Nations: 5 appearances

Steve Jones

Jabba, as we call him, is a great footballer and does things that other hookers cannot even dream of doing. His attitude throughout the Championship was first class and I cannot speak highly enough of him.

2005 Six Nations: 0 appearances

Gareth Llewellyn

At the end of last season I persuaded Gareth to carry on for one more season. He did that and we were grateful to have him around the camp this season.

2005 Six Nations: 0 appearances

Hal Luscombe

I've got a lot of time for Hal having worked with him at the Dragons. He is an effective player both in attack and defence. Unfortunately, a knee injury curtailed his Championship.

2005 Six Nations: 3 appearances

Dwayne Peel

A lot of people have commented on how Dwayne has taken off this season. I share that view. He is our tap-and-go captain and is without doubt one of the nicest guys you will ever meet.

2005 Six Nations: 5 appearances

Robin McBryde

I worked with Robin at Swansea in 1991, so we go back a long way. I couldn't keep him at Swansea because Garin Jenkins was there and Robin wouldn't play second fiddle to anyone. He did the right thing going to Llanelli and fourteen years on he has proved himself to be crucial to our forward effort.

2005 Six Nations: 4 appearances

Kevin Morgan

I am delighted for him. He has been through a great deal in terms of injuries, but he has battled back to become a key member of the squad.

2005 Six Nations: 5 appearances

Michael Owen

When I took over everyone was telling me he was a second row. I didn't believe it and had no real intention of playing him anywhere else than no.8. He has come on as a footballer and can be proud of the way he handled matters as captain after Gareth Thomas was ruled out. A pleasure to work with such a knowledgeable young man.

2005 Six Nations: 5 appearances

Sonny Parker

All I can say about Sonny is that he was desperately unlucky. He had a good summer tour and Autumn Series before suffering a stinger injury which meant we were without him until the Ireland match.

2005 Six Nations: 0 appearances

Michael Phillips

Outstanding, on and off the field. His chances have been limited but his performance in the North v South game at Twickenham provided further confirmation of his world class ability.

2005 Six Nations: 0 appearances

Richie Pugh

A brilliant young prospect who might have got his chance had it not have been for the form of others. Another contender for the summer tour and a player who has already proven himself to be the fastest forward in the history of Welsh rugby.

2005 Six Nations: 0 appearances

Tom Shanklin

Tom is enjoyable to work with, a real team man. I gave him a chance in the A team a few years back and asked Graham Henry to select him in the senior side. He has always had a spark, but this season that spark became a flame.

2005 Six Nations: 5 appearances

Robert Sidoli

Sid found it tough after undergoing surgery on his groin in the summer and when he came back to play for the Blues I told him that he needed to improve. He did that and made it impossible for me to leave him out for the England game. Since then his performances have been out of the top drawer and has proven to be a great line out leader.

2005 Six Nations: 5 appearances

Robin Sowden-Taylor

Robin was a late addition to the squad after Colin Charvis was injured, but he came on to win a cap and proved to me that he has what it takes. A real contender for the summer tour and I have no doubt that he will be back for some more Six Nations action in the future.

2005 Six Nations: 1 appearance

Ceri Sweeney

I have a huge amount of time for Ceri even though he destroyed me as chairman of the fines committee. He is a great young player who will be around on the international stage for many years to come.

2005 Six Nations: 3 appearances

Mark Taylor

I signed Mark from Pontypool in 1994 and 10 years later he is still playing incredibly well. He has had a difficult time with injuries and illness but look at the game against Ireland, he was faultless.

2005 Six Nations: 1 appearance

Gareth Thomas

Magnificent. Gareth was an example to his fellow players, both on and off the field, proving to be a catalyst for the collective team spirit that prevailed throughout the competition. I have to give myself a pat on the back for picking him as captain.

2005 Six Nations: 3 appearances

Jonathan Thomas

A real gentleman and a great guy to be with. He is developing superbly as an international player and showed throughout the Championship that he is a true athlete. Unlucky to lose his spot but carried himself with huge dignity.

2005 Six Nations: 4 appearances

Martyn Williams

What can I say about Martyn that has not already been said. He stayed behind in the summer on our request and although he didn't play in the autumn series, he came in to the side in February and was fully deserving of his man of the series award. Fantastic.

2005 Six Nations: 5 appearances

Rhys Williams

I am so pleased for Rhys. He missed the England game through injury and because of that lost a little ground. However, having battled back into contention, he was fantastic against France and deserved his try in Scotland. He certainly proved a few people wrong.

2005 Six Nations: 2 appearances

Shane Williams

Simply awesome. There is little doubt that Shane provided some of the Six Nations' magic moments. His try against England, break against Italy and his try-scoring pass against France were three of the best moments.

2005 Six Nations: 5 appearances

John Yapp

A great prospect. I looked closely at him in the Autumn and had no doubt that he was ready for international rugby. He has great desire and he never once let us down.

2005 Six Nations: 5 appearances

And the rest...

Just a mention to the support staff - you were all a pleasure to work with and each and every one proved to me once again that there is no I in team. Well done and thanks.

Clive Griffiths, Scott Johnson, Andrew Hore, Mark Bennett, Dan King, Mick Wadsworth, Caroline Morgan, Alan Phillips, Alun Carter, Rhodri Bown, Mark Davies, Prof. John Williams, Dr Roger Evans, John Rowlands, Simon Rimmer, Stuart Evans, Alun Donovan, Geraint John, Leigh Jones, Andy Moore, Shaun Holly and Gareth Jenkins.

MIKE RUDDOCK

Vision Sports Publishing

2 Coombe Gardens,

London, SW20 0QU

www.visionsp.co.uk

This First Edition Published by Vision Sports Publishing in 2005

Printed and bound in Italy by Printer Trento Srl

Paper is 150gsm Gardamatt Art

A CIP catalogue record for this book is available from the British Library

ISBN 0-9546428-8-0

acknowledgements

ACKNOWLEDGEMENTS

THE BREATHING FIRE! TEAM

Managing Editors: Jim Drewett & Toby Trotman

Editor: Paul Morgan

Words: Graham Clutton

Design: Neal Cobourne, rkidesign@btinternet.com

Team Wales representation: Richard Harry,

Mark Spoors, Louise Hewitt

All pictures by:

HUW EVANS PICTURE AGENCY

Photographers:

Huw Evans, Gareth Everett,

Matthew Phillips, James Davies

www.welshrugbypics.co.uk

WITH THANKS TO...

VISION SPORTS PUBLISHING

First and foremost our thanks to Mike Ruddock and the entire Welsh rugby squad for their sensational and well-deserved Grand Slam. To Mark Spoors of Big Red Management and Richard Harry of Team Wales for letting us loose on the project in this of all years, and to Huw Evans, Gareth Everett, Matthew Phillips and James Davies from the Huw Evans Picture Agency in Cardiff for embracing the concept and delivering some truly stunning sports photography.

To Paul Morgan and Graham Clutton for working round the clock on the words, to Neal Cobourne for his fantastic design work, and to Andy Webb, Claire Thompson and all at Turnaround Publisher Services for getting the book in the shops. Special thanks also to the WRU for allowing Huw and the team access to the inner sanctums of the Welsh team, and especially Alan Phillips for his enthusiasm for the project and invaluable assistance from day one.

HUW EVANS PICTURE AGENCY

Huw Evans Picture Agency would like to thank the Wales team and management for their co-operation during the season and the honour of being allowed such unparalleled access to such a great bunch of guys! To both captains for their ideas, and Rhys Williams for his expertise behind the camera (*don't give up rugby Rhys*).

Also to WRU Travel and Robert Davies Travel for getting us to the venues, Paul Morgan for his infectious enthusiasm, the publishers for their 'great idea', Simon Rimmer the team press officer for trying to get into all the pictures and Liz Jones the WRU press officer for getting us past all the 'helpful stewards' into the changing rooms. Last but not least JR the kitman for making us load all the luggage in Edinburgh.

We, as the players, would like to thank the following:

First of all Mike Ruddock and the backroom staff, who made every day during the Six Nations campaign an enjoyable one and without their commitment to the cause as well as their passion for a Welsh rugby team to be successful we would not be where we are today. Along with Mike the following were instrumental in the success: Clive Griffiths, Scott Johnson, Andrew Hore, Mark Bennett, Dan King, Mick Wadsworth, Caroline Morgan, Alan Phillips, Alun Carter, Rhodri Bown, Mark Davies, Prof. John Williams, Dr Roger Evans, John Rowlands, Simon Rimmer, Stuart Evans, Alun Donovan, Geraint John, Leigh Jones, Andy Moore, Shaun Holly and Gareth Jenkins.

We would like to thank Richard Harry at the WRPA who has always been around with advice and a friendly smile whenever needed. We have dedicated this book, which we are incredibly proud of, in loving memory of Richard's beautiful wife Leanne who sadly passed away on 29th March 2005.

Without Mark Spoors at Big Red Management we would not be thanking anyone as he has made 'Breathing Fire' a reality. Mark is the driving force behind 'Team Wales' and we hope he will be for many more victorious campaigns to come.

We would also like to thank the WRU, and especially Alan Phillips and Paul Thorburn, for allowing the book to go ahead and their support throughout.

Also Huw Evans and his team of merry men who made the book come to life with the amazing photographs which you have just seen, and also Jim and Toby at Vision Sports Publishing for having faith in us when other publishing houses did not.

Finally, and most importantly, we would like to thank you, the fans. You are without doubt the greatest fans in the world. From memories of 40,000 of you drinking Edinburgh dry on that amazing day, to the tears of joy after the Ireland game, we did it all for you. We hope that you enjoy our book about the most amazing two months in any of our lives. We enjoyed being there, and hope that you can enjoy these fantastic memories.

TEAM
WALES